MEN'S SUITS! 25% OFF!

CARTOONS CREATED TO KEEP YOU IN STITCHES!

FASHIONED BY ROY SCHLEMME

(100% OFF!!!)

AuthorHouse™ LLC
1663 Liberty Drive
Bloomington, IN 47403
www.authorhouse.com
Phone: 1-800-839-8640

Published by AuthorHouse   10/01/2013

ISBN: 978-1-4918-1030-9 (sc)
ISBN: 978-1-4918-1029-3 (e)

Library of Congress Control Number: 2013915107

For the Staten Island Cirbuses...
Dickie & Pat.

R.SCHLEMME

For those who enjoy being stared at!

If you are one of the few, rare individuals who might
find themselves somewhat unnerved by having been made
the focus of 49 boggle-eyed birds, then I suggest a
time-tested, simple remedy. Turn to the next page immediately
and continue turning slowly and methodically until you've
gotten to page 131. At that point, you'll have reached a state
of total relaxation and ultimate enjoyment. And furthermore,
during the process, I guarantee none of my cartoons
will be staring at you...at least, not intentionally!

—*Roy Schlemme*

"Think screaming-crowd, high-pressure, 10-meter Olympic diving finals, Corey."

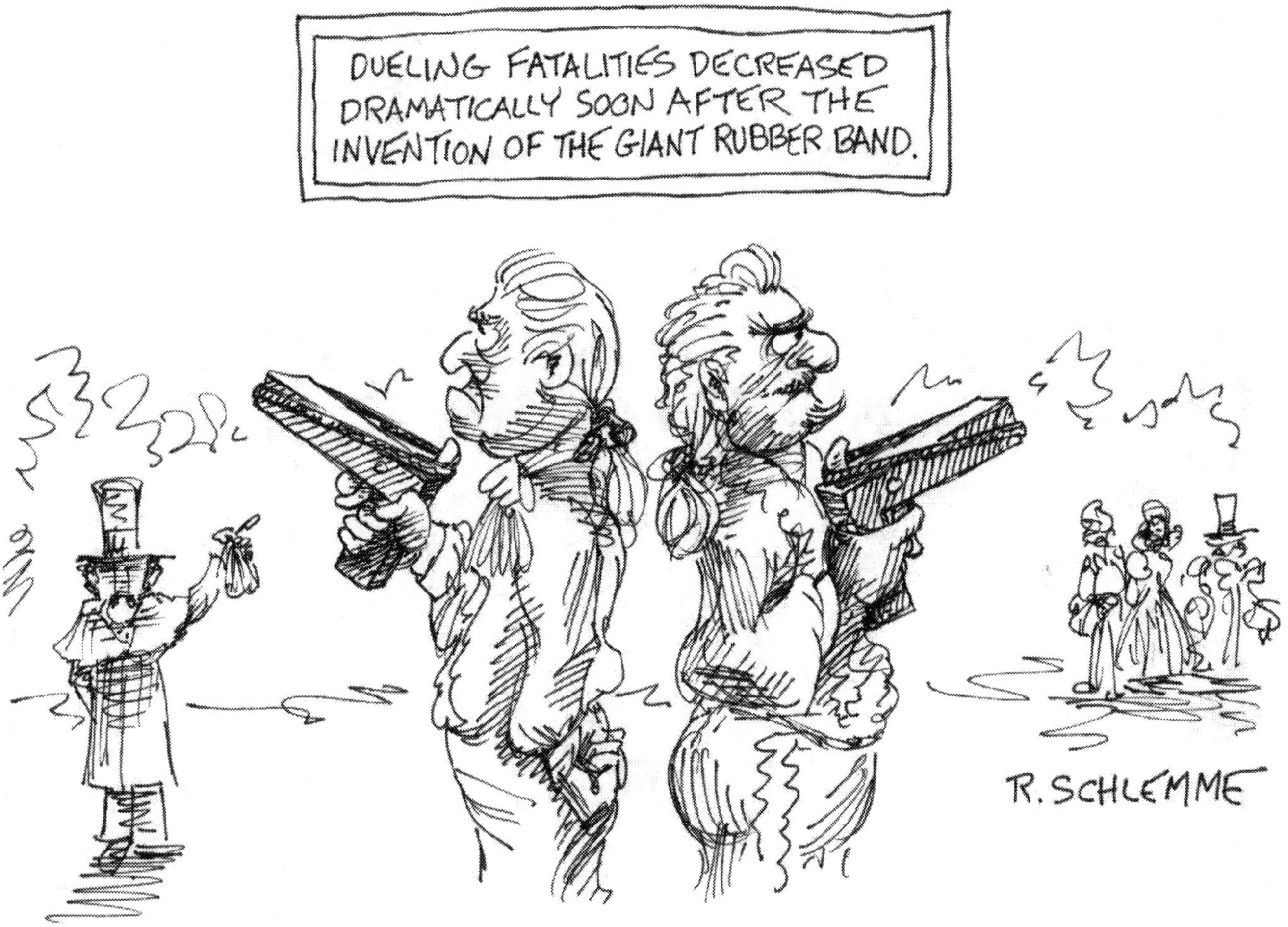
DUELING FATALITIES DECREASED DRAMATICALLY SOON AFTER THE INVENTION OF THE GIANT RUBBER BAND.
R. SCHLEMME

"Ever notice how some artists always seem to generate more expressive responses than others?"

R. SCHLEMME

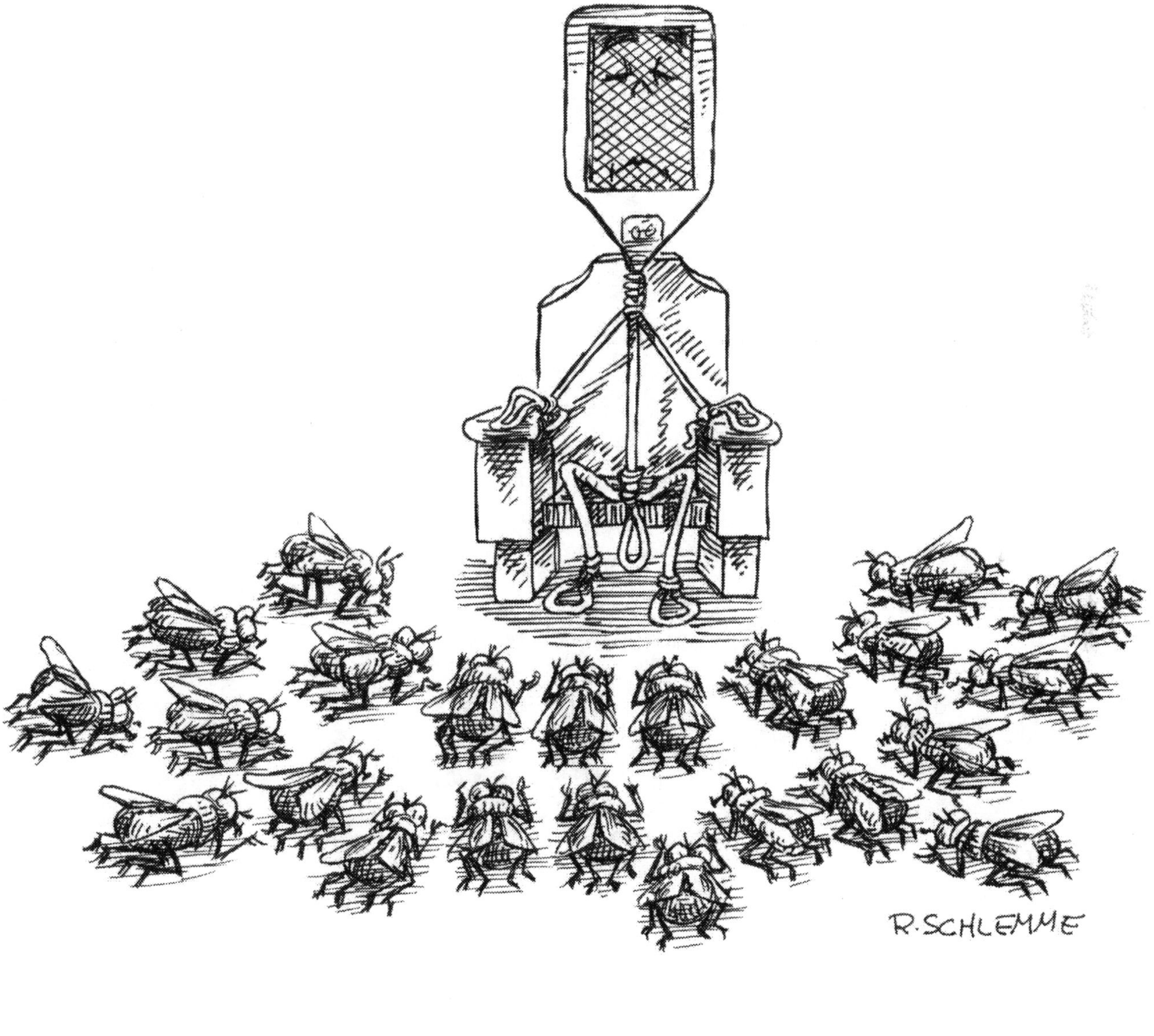
R.SCHLEMME

"Even if my original experiment tanks, we'll,
at least, come out of it with a novelty toaster."

"If we wind up getting our butts whipped,
do they erect a 'less-than-triumphal' arch?"

"Granted, store traffic is down by 38%,
but shoplifting's dropped by a whopping 95%."

"Looks like the larval stage just got in."

R. SCHLEMME

Seesaw for acrophobics.

R. SCHLEMME

"Save!"

R. SCHLEMME

"Sludgemann, I don't know what your
former employer's policy was, but, around here,
we frown on hallway slime trails."

"I still prefer *'The end is near!'*."

R. SCHLEMME

"Should I stop back later
or just work around you?"

R. SCHLEMME

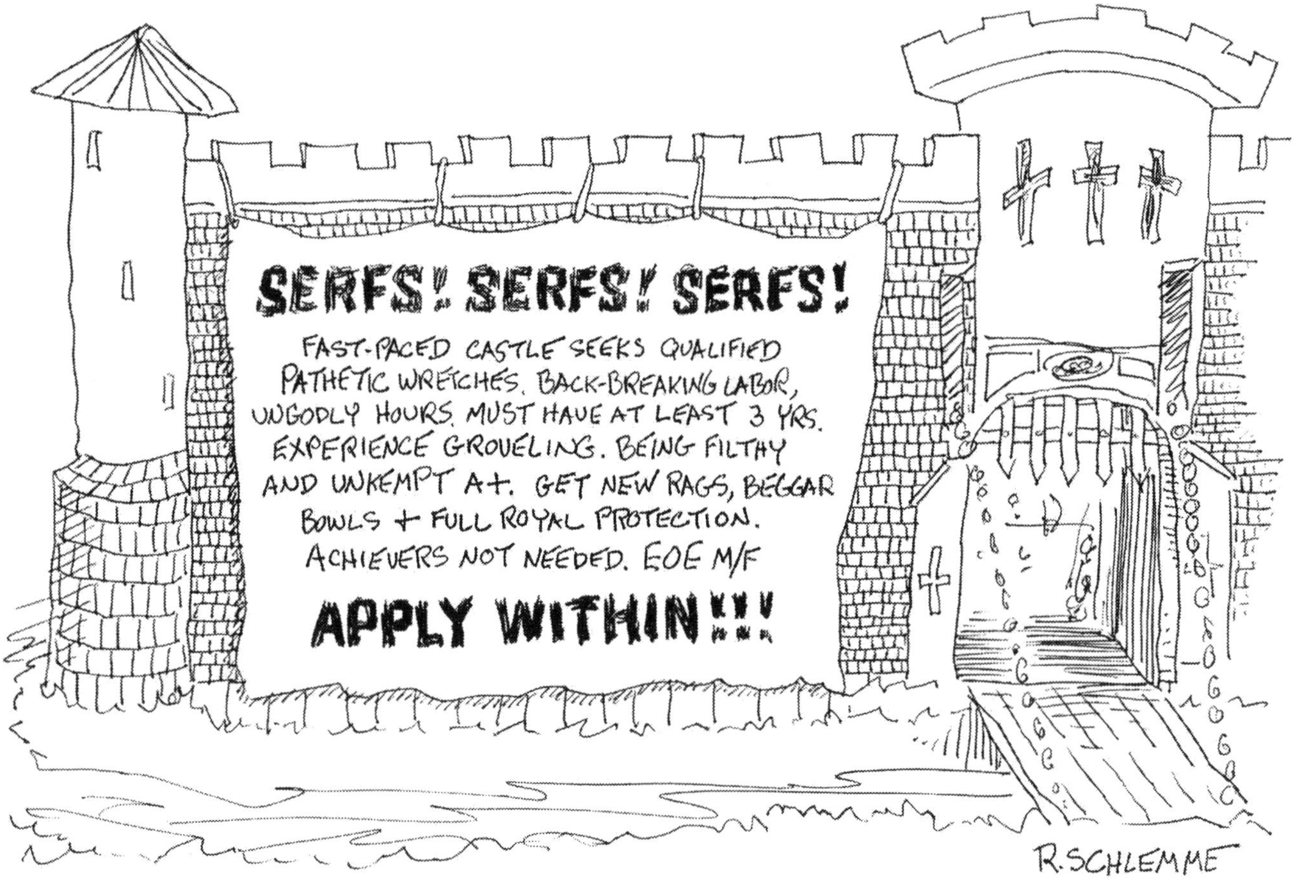
SERFS! SERFS! SERFS!
FAST-PACED CASTLE SEEKS QUALIFIED PATHETIC WRETCHES. BACK-BREAKING LABOR, UNGODLY HOURS. MUST HAVE AT LEAST 3 YRS. EXPERIENCE GROVELING. BEING FILTHY AND UNKEMPT A+. GET NEW RAGS, BEGGAR BOWLS + FULL ROYAL PROTECTION. ACHIEVERS NOT NEEDED. EOE M/F
APPLY WITHIN!!!
R. SCHLEMME

"Almost closing time! Drink up, everybody!"

"All I remember is the bright, blue glow
it emitted just before I shot it."

R. SCHLEMME

HAND SIGNALS.

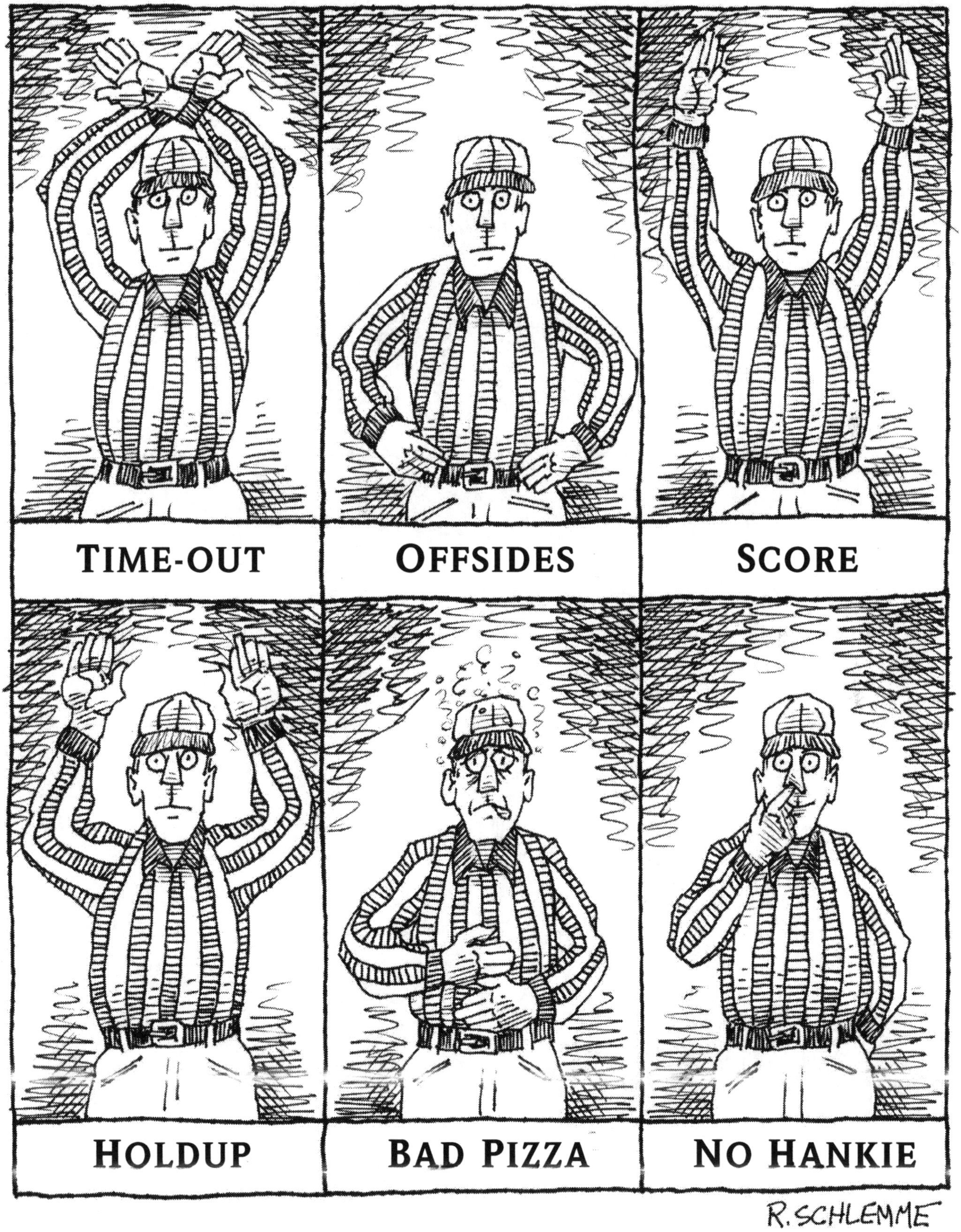
TIME-OUT
OFFSIDES
SCORE
HOLDUP
BAD PIZZA
NO HANKIE
R. SCHLEMME

"You're no fun anymore."

R. SCHLEMME

R. SCHLEMME

"I'd bet heavily against fitting
a square pig in a round hole.

On pointe.

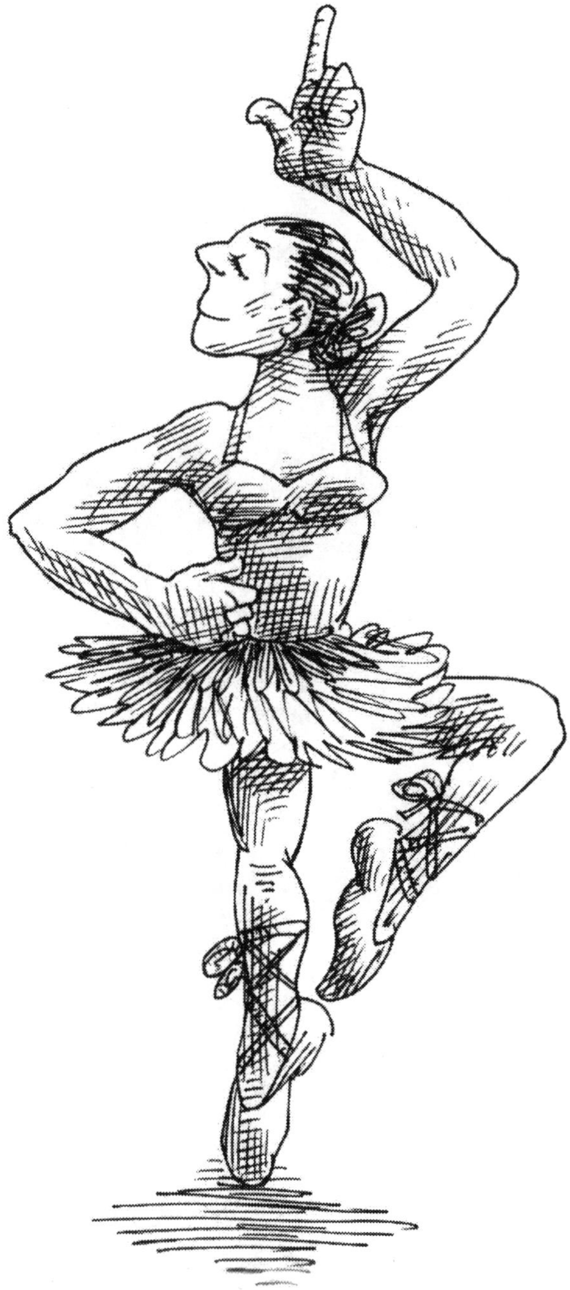

On pills.

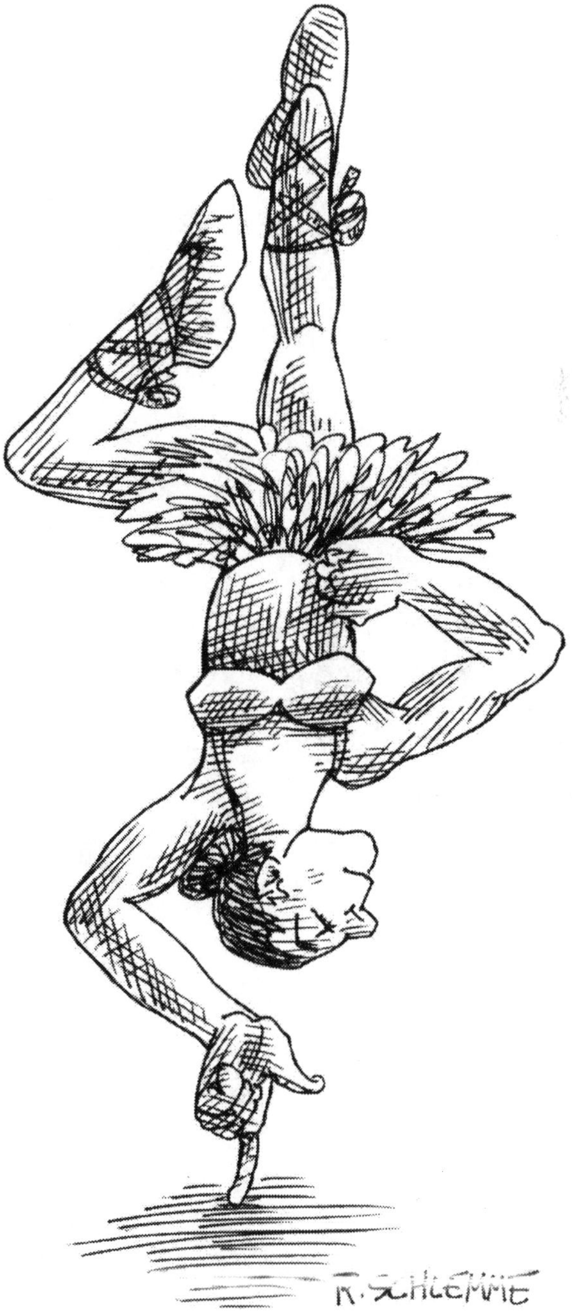
R. SCHLEMME

"Things <u>have</u> improved around here.
Now I'm counting more dead flies than live
ones on their window ledges."

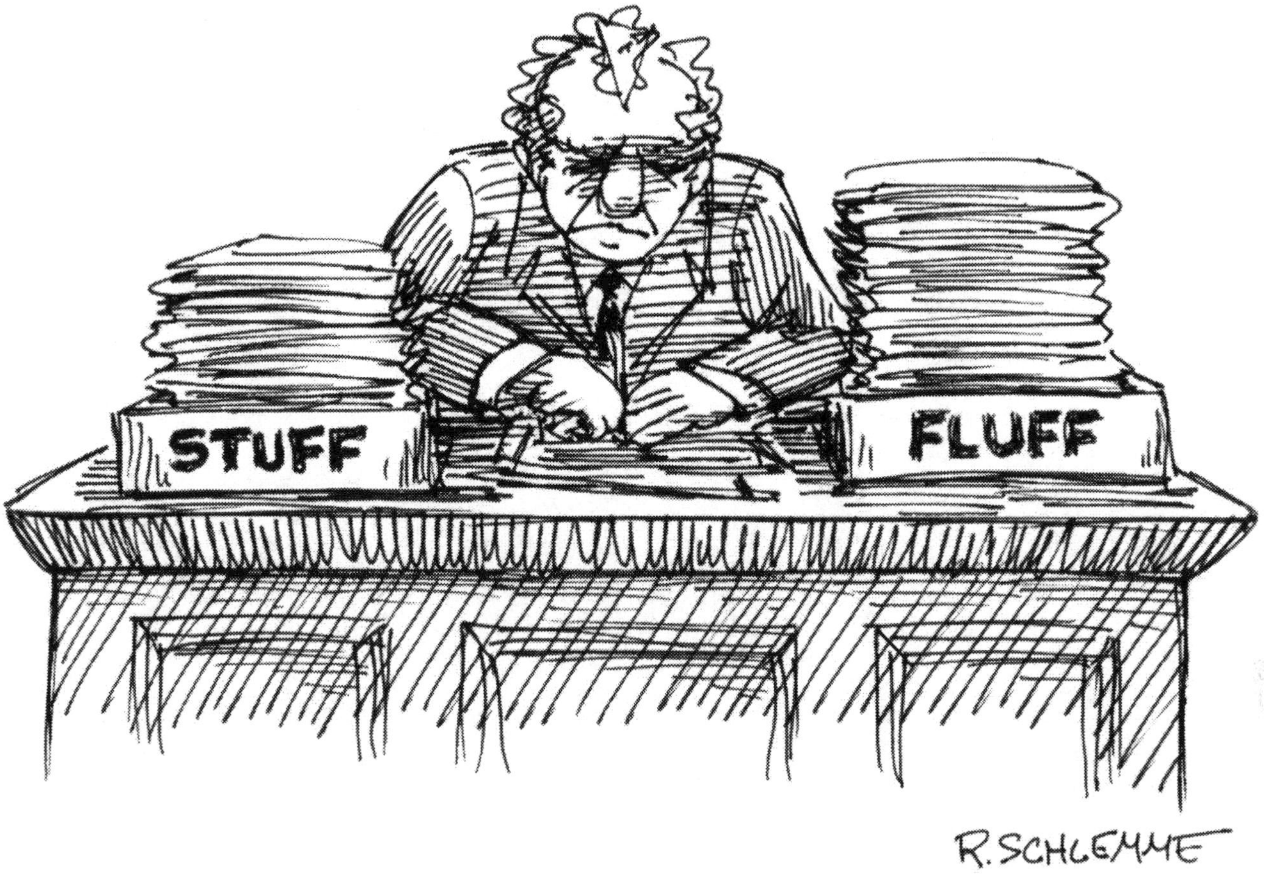
STUFF
FLUFF
R. SCHLEMME

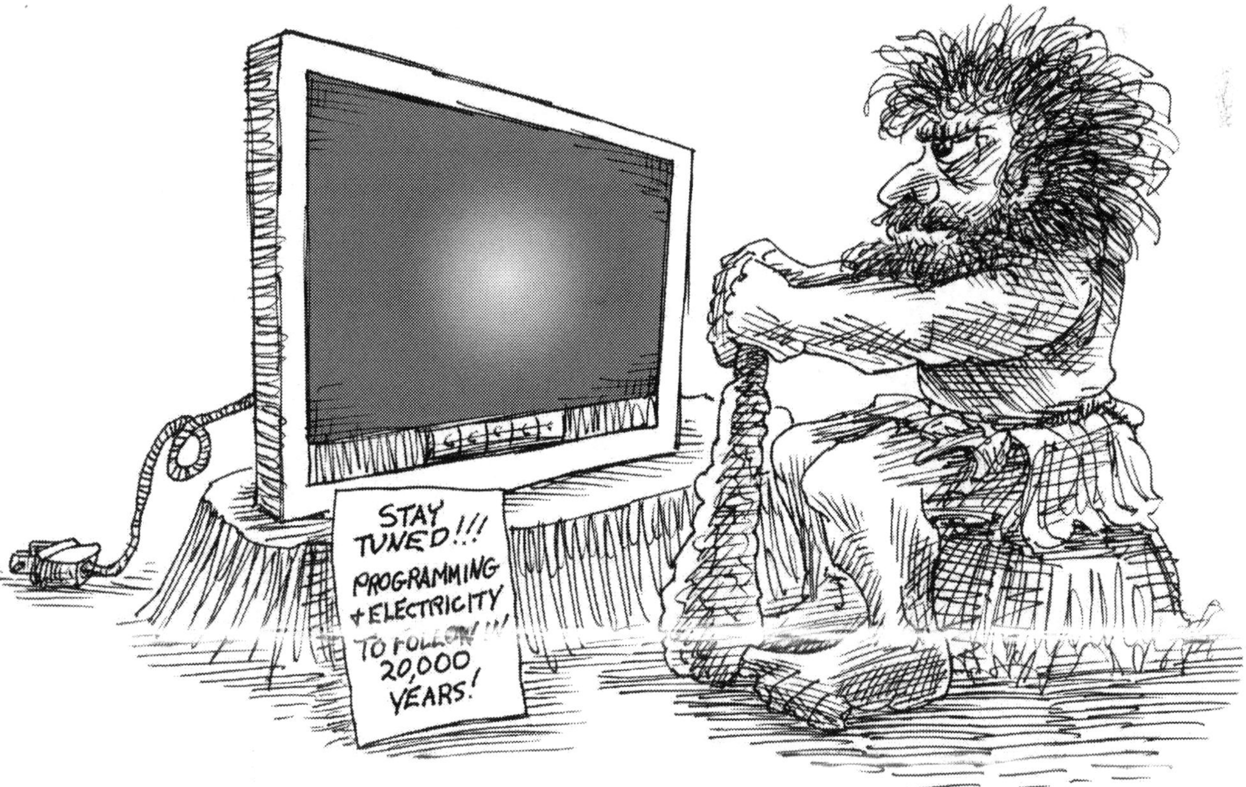
STAY TUNED!!!
PROGRAMMING + ELECTRICITY TO FOLLOW IN 20,000 YEARS!
R. SCHLEMME

"Mom, it followed us home.
Can we keep it?"

"Thanks so much. We really
enjoyed the cast party for
your new claymation feature."

R. SCHLEMME

"...with custody of all the sable hair brushes getting awarded to..."

R. SCHLEMME

"At times, I regret having married an optimist."

R. SCHLEMME

FOR SALE

ONLY DRIVEN ALTERNATE LIGHT YEARS IN THIS QUADRANT BY A 700 YR. OLD CALTERIAN GRANNY.

R. SCHLEMME

"Is Donny asleep yet, Ms. Mills?
We'd like to haunt his dreams."

"Beyond your first three rows,
I'm sure the audience will be able to
focus on the magic of Mozart."

R. SCHLEMME

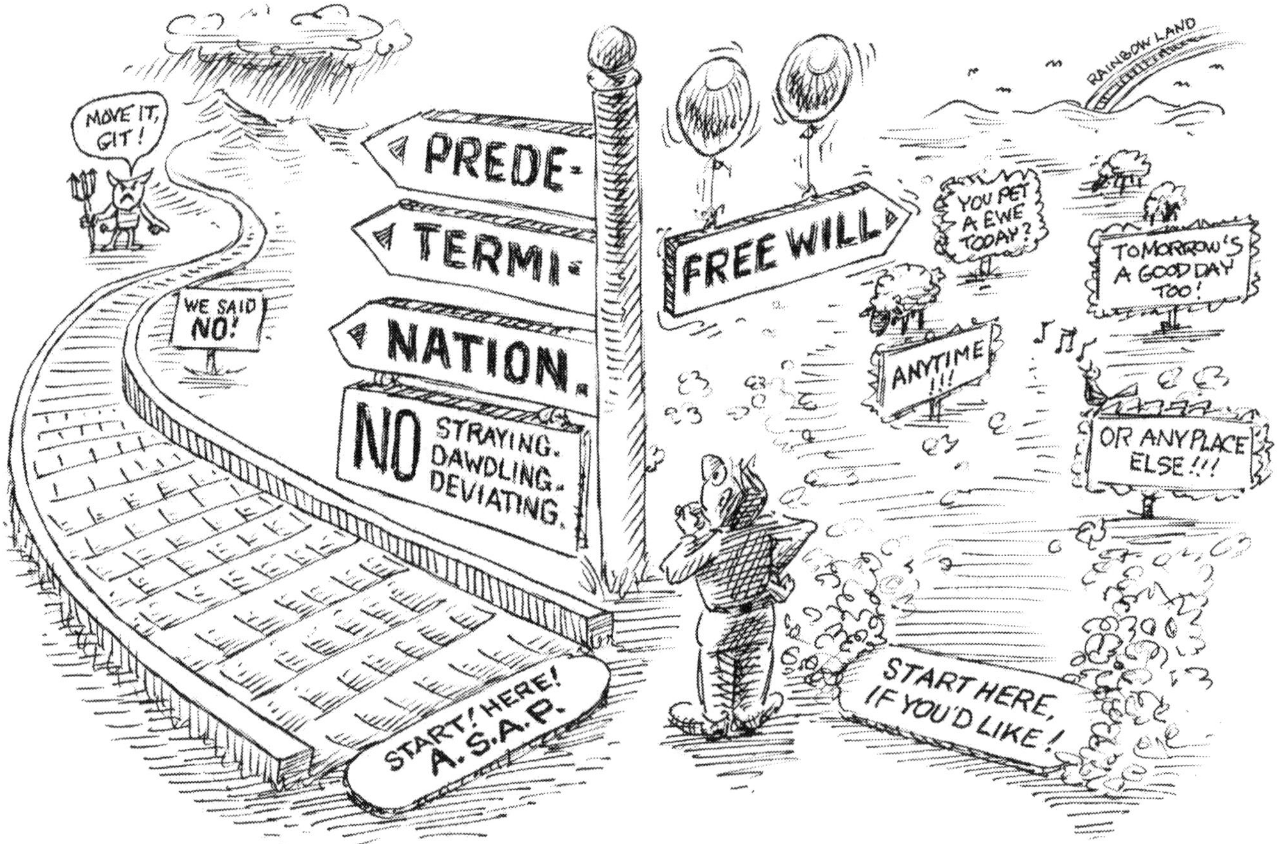
MOVE IT, GIT!
WE SAID NO!
PREDE-
TERMI-
NATION.
NO STRAYING. DAWDLING. DEVIATING.
FREE WILL
YOU PET A EWE TODAY?
RAINBOW LAND
TOMORROW'S A GOOD DAY TOO!
ANYTIME !!!
OR ANY PLACE ELSE !!!
START! HERE! A.S.A.P.
START HERE, IF YOU'D LIKE!
R. SCHLEMME

"...and to all those who voted for me because I looked
so electable in a three-piece suit...SURPRISE!"

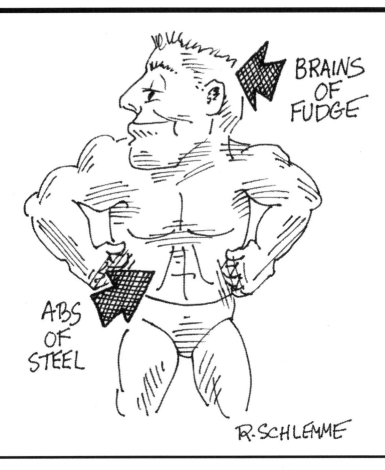

The captain turned his ship to port, narrowly missing a nasty accident with the chablis.

Straphangers.

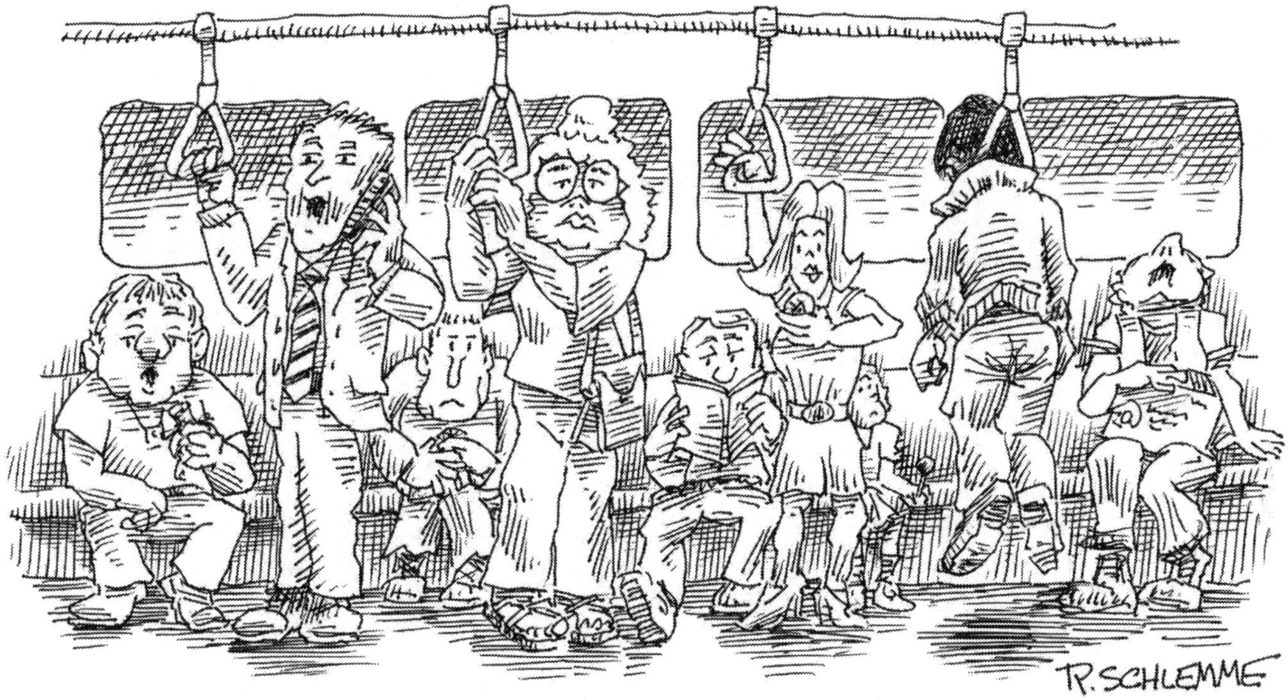
R. SCHLEMME

"What a nave! What an apse! What a great place to do my Yankee Stadium PA announcer giving today's lineup!"

R. SCHLEMME

"...and to think we almost missed
our baby making her first peep."

R. SCHLEMME

"Sure, you give, but not unless
it gets squeezed out of you."

"Think we might get to your
surprise finish a bit faster?"

"I gotta admit, it's a unique way to
lure our *'Weight Loss Club'* members
into the running program."

"What if I keep stealing from the rich, but then,
offer the poor loans at very attractive rates?"

"...so do you, 'P', from this day forward
take 'H', within the bonds of proper pronunciation,
in union as a phonetically sounded 'F'?"

"To be safe, we really should
think about boiling it first."

"It's OK now, but wait till they morph
into frogs keeping us awake with
booming all-night concerts."

"When you get to this end, you'll really
enjoy the cute puppy with a blue collar."

R.SCHLEMME

"Is it ever possible to overdo wallowing?"

"Hey, remind management about a certain promise
to have me out and gone by the holidays!"

R. SCHLEMME

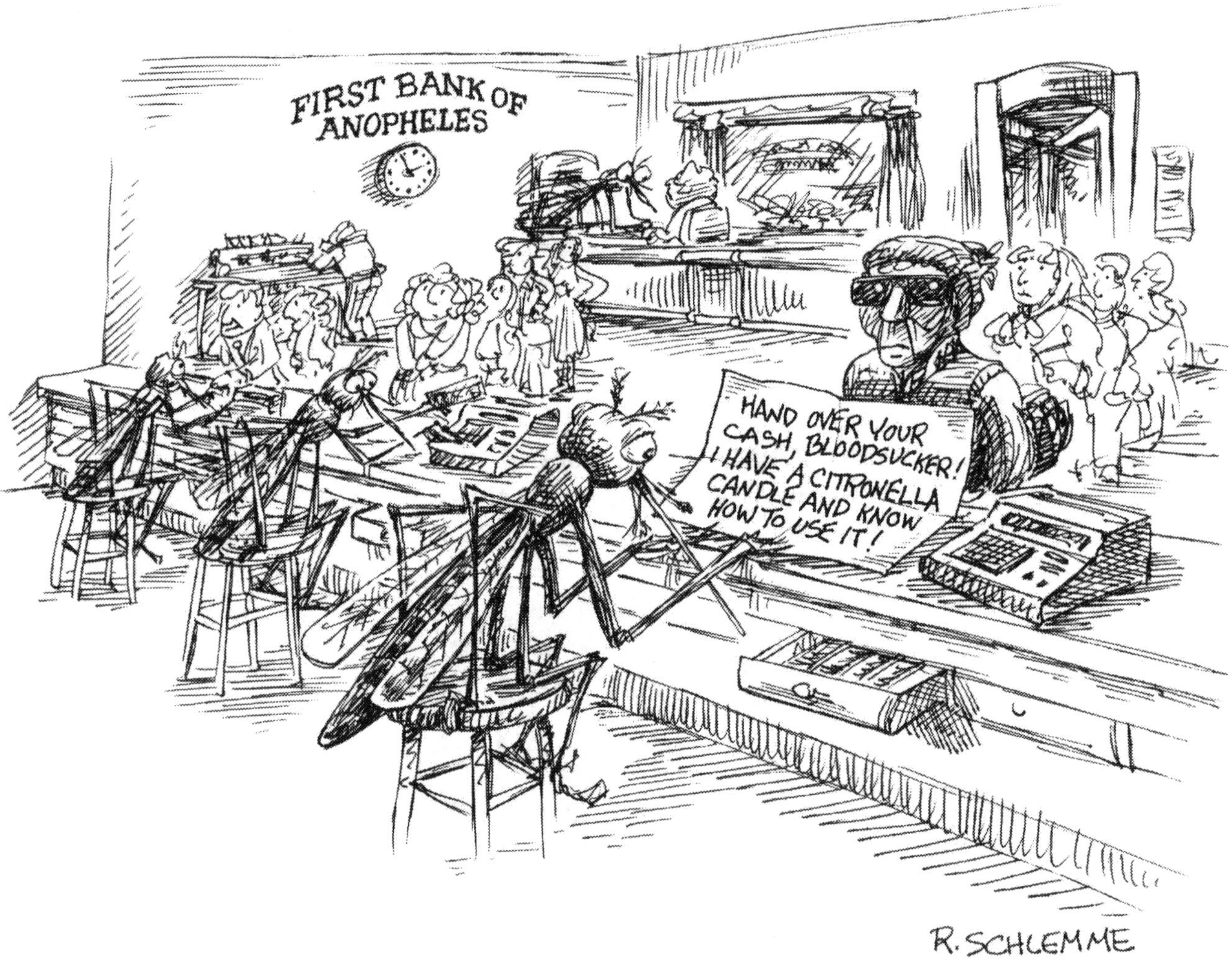
FIRST BANK OF ANOPHELES
HAND OVER YOUR CASH, BLOODSUCKER! I HAVE A CITRONELLA CANDLE AND KNOW HOW TO USE IT!
R. SCHLEMME

"It should heal nicely, Mr. Pinocchio...
unless, of course, you resume lying again."

"At these prices, I usually get to choose how I'd like to have them prepared."

"A big nuisance to tote around,
but it always gets me safely
across the interstate."

"Why couldn't you have done stone lions like every other self-involved man-child in the neighborhood?"

"It's simple, it's efficient, and it's going
to totally change our world!
I call it *'The Lazy Susan'*!"

"Remember, if things don't pan out here,
I get first dibs on the boots."

R. SCHLEMME

"Mom always encouraged me to participate in the political process."

R·SCHLEMME

All-Zombie Gymnastics Team.

"Sorry, your majesty. I can't process
an order of just 'sugar-to-go'."

"Yosemite information? Yes, ma'am!
By that little cave over where
those other cars are parked."

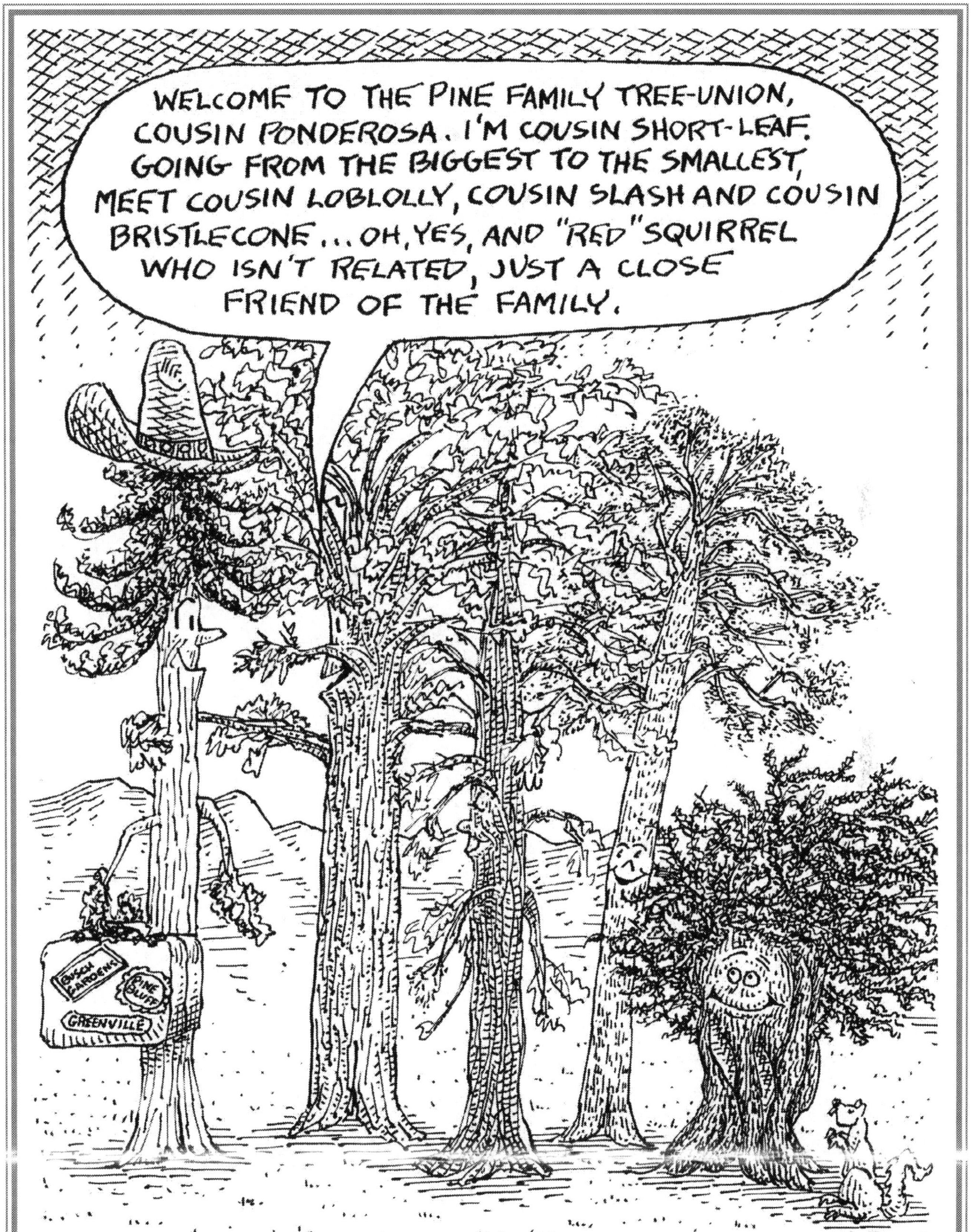
WELCOME TO THE PINE FAMILY TREE-UNION, COUSIN PONDEROSA. I'M COUSIN SHORT-LEAF. GOING FROM THE BIGGEST TO THE SMALLEST, MEET COUSIN LOBLOLLY, COUSIN SLASH AND COUSIN BRISTLECONE... OH, YES, AND "RED" SQUIRREL WHO ISN'T RELATED, JUST A CLOSE FRIEND OF THE FAMILY.
BUSCH GARDENS
PINE BLUFF
GREENVILLE
R.SCHLEMME

"Applaud, Lowell...
the concert's finito, not pause-o!"

R.SCHLEMME

R.SCHLEMME

"To Fame & Fortune... and fast!"

"You're telling me this is really
<u>our</u> *'Little cabin in the woods...
ideal for a small family'*?"

"So, sweetie, which of my soon-to-be
disinherited relations suggested you
suck up to the decrepit money machine?"

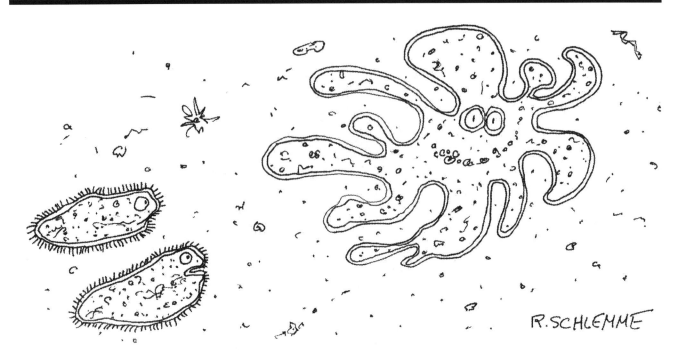

"Gelatinous exhibitionism
turns me off!"

"Scrooge, try that line again.
It's still coming out *'Baaa, humbug!'*."

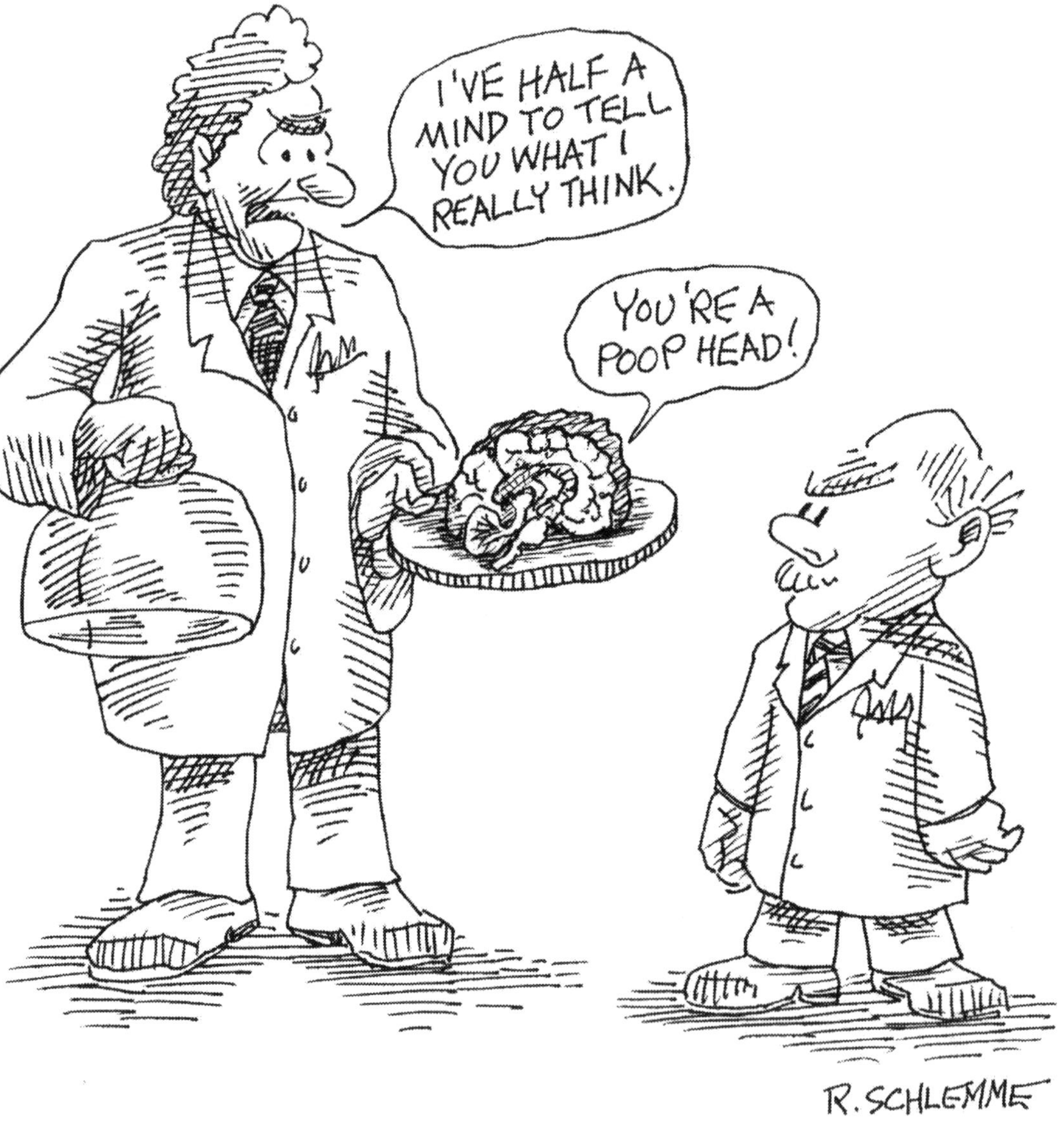
I'VE HALF A MIND TO TELL YOU WHAT I REALLY THINK.
YOU'RE A POOP HEAD!
R. SCHLEMME

"Dear, must you play poker
with the boys every night?"

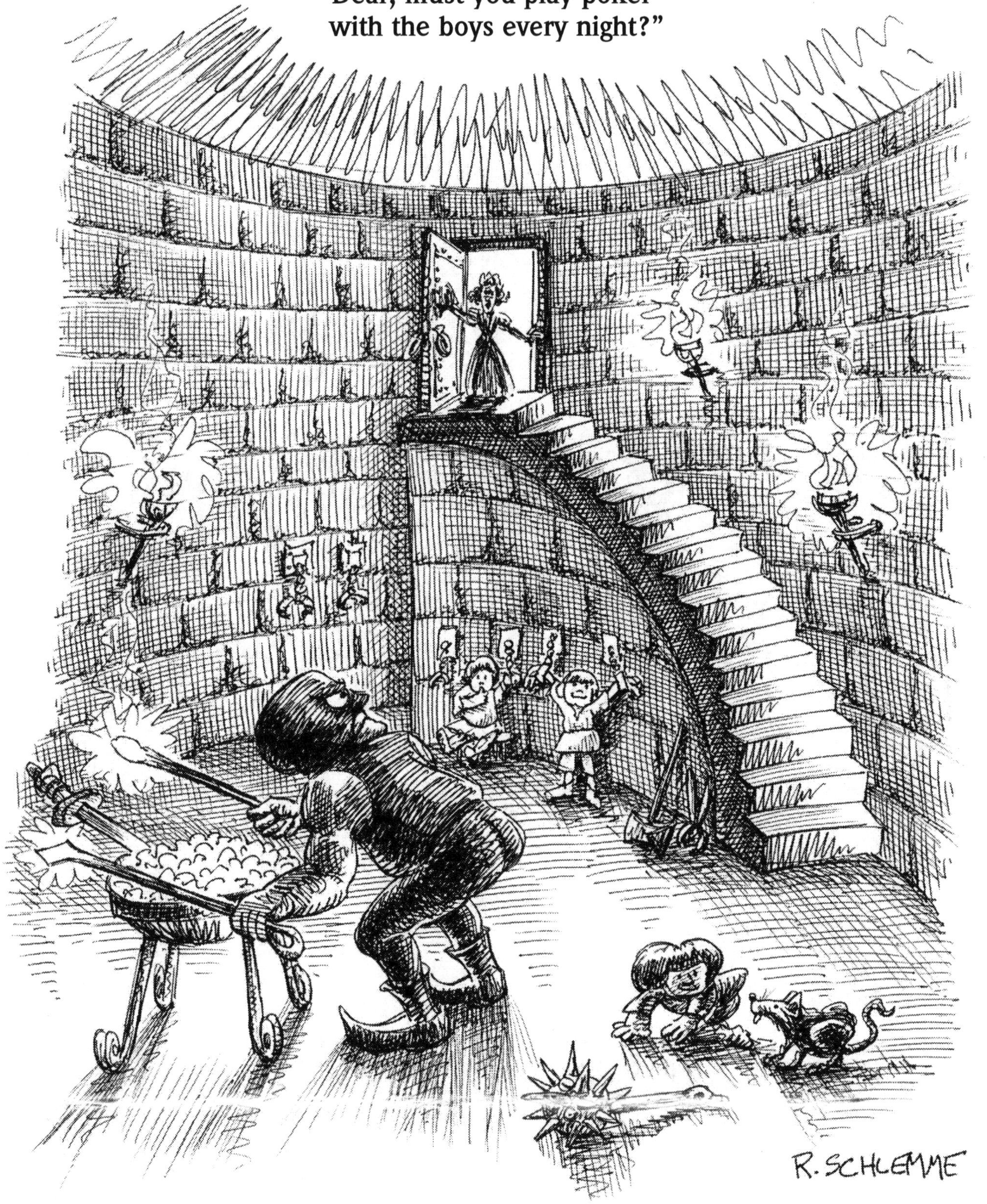
R. SCHLEMME

"...and what was the reason for
leaving your last very large dog?"

"We don't mind you bringing lunch on board.
Just don't toss those peels in the aisle
when you're finished."

R. SCHLEMME

"If makin' baked bean necklaces
ain't the dumbest job ever, I'll be danged
if'n I kin figger out whut might be."

"That's my spot!"

"You really shouldn't allow yourself to be consumed by hate."

"Hey, gang...titanic marine insurance claim
bearing down off the port bow!"

"You should know, there's a nominal surcharge
for garments with extra appendages."

Blinding beauty.

"Unfortunately, it can't take the weight, sir.
I must request that you drain our pool."

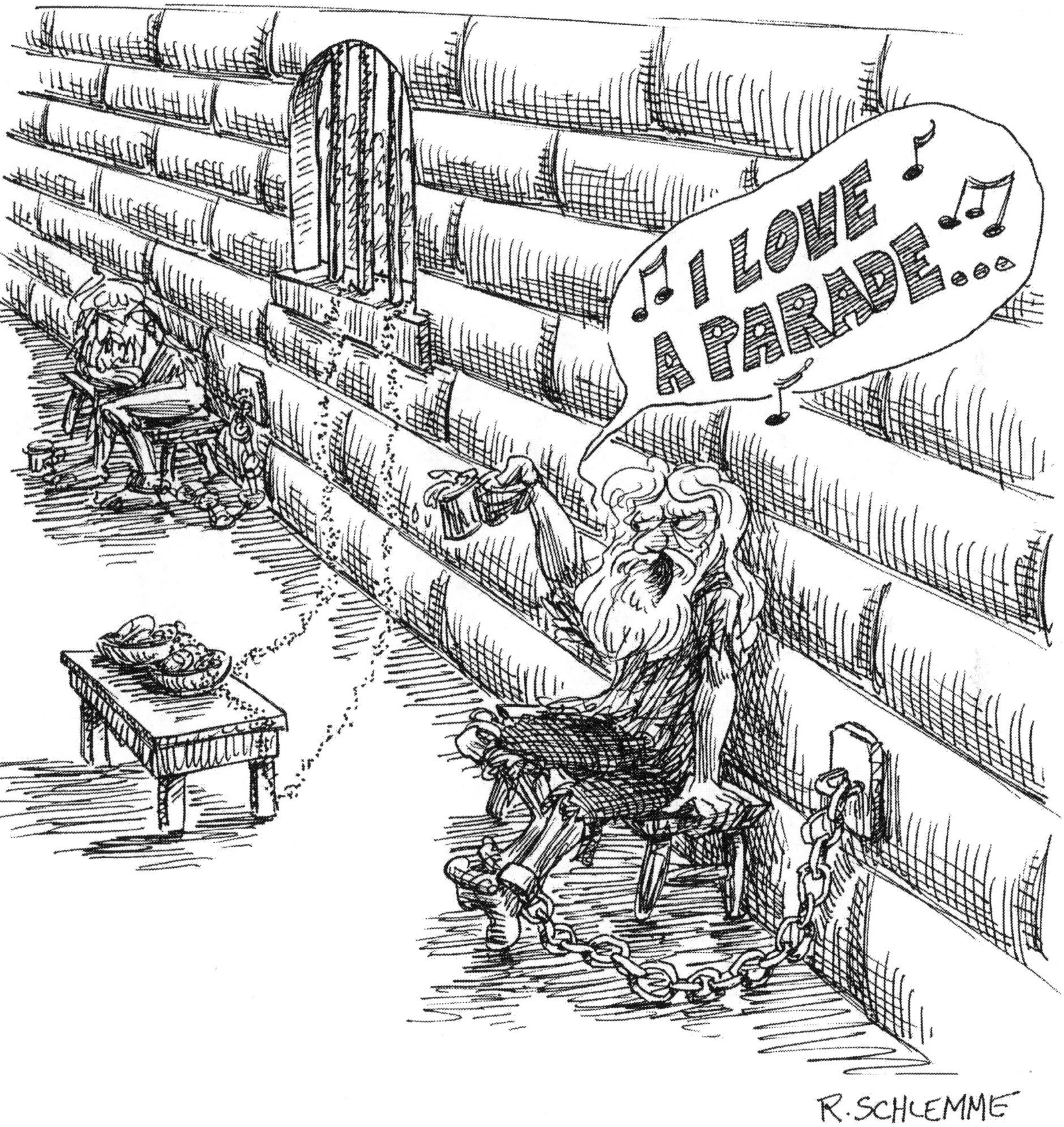
I LOVE A PARADE...
R. SCHLEMME

R. SCHLEMME

"So much for our little town's
budding pacifist movement."

"Frankly, Leo, I don't think
the Renaissance is ready
for sardonic humor."

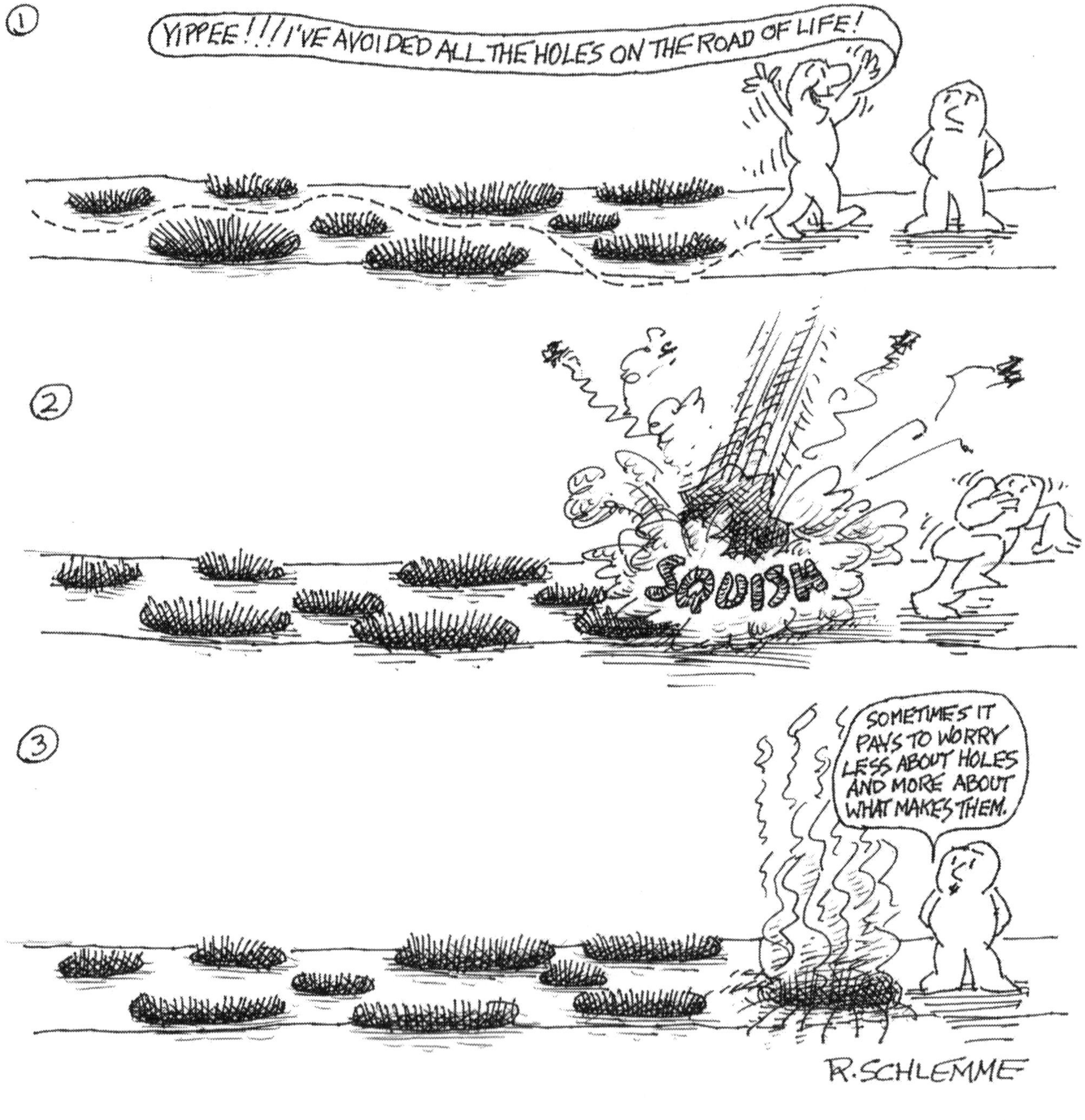
1
YIPPEE!!!! I'VE AVOIDED ALL THE HOLES ON THE ROAD OF LIFE!
2
SQUISH
3
SOMETIMES IT PAYS TO WORRY LESS ABOUT HOLES AND MORE ABOUT WHAT MAKES THEM.
R. SCHLEMME

"How inconsiderate...making yourself
a fudge sundae without offering
to make me one, too."

"Stay calm, precious! Just redo whatever
you did originally, only in reverse order!"

"Kill that frilly border, recolor the field azure and
change those 'Swans in repose' to 'Lions rampant'...
then we might discuss 'sale' here."

"The *'truite meunière aux herbes'* is exceptional...
and, I believe, a bit still remains of what
I was unable to finish at lunch."

"A self-confident candle never sweats."

"Stop bristling at each other...
or I'll have to paste you both."

R. SCHLEMME

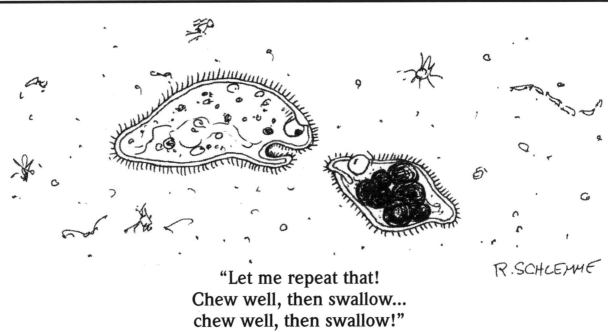

R. SCHLEMME

"Let me repeat that!
Chew well, then swallow...
chew well, then swallow!"

"I was told to be prepared
for a surprise 'happy ending'."

"...and at today's closing bell, we find
Guinness down almost four pints."

"I never question methodology, only results."

R. SCHLEMME

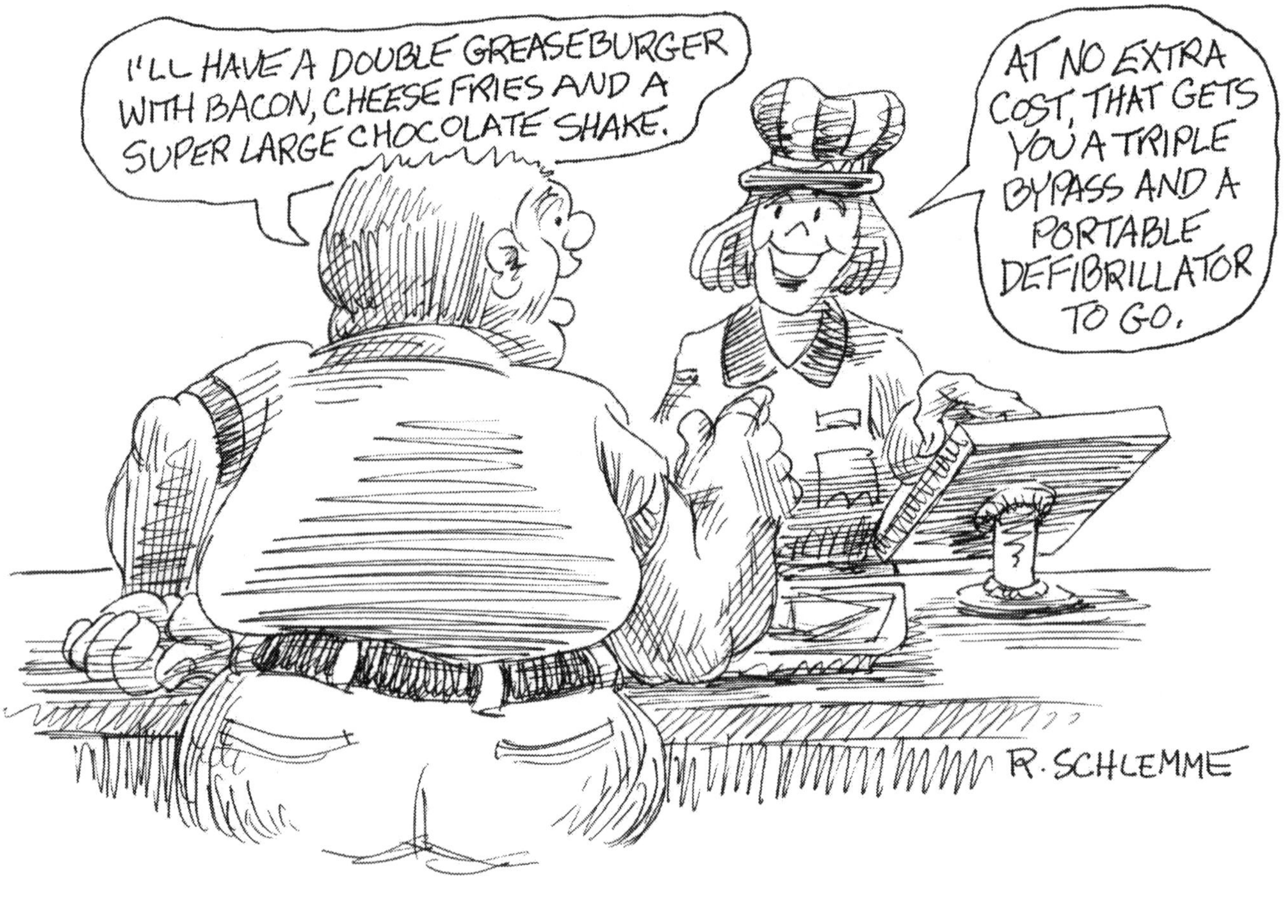
I'LL HAVE A DOUBLE GREASEBURGER WITH BACON, CHEESE FRIES AND A SUPER LARGE CHOCOLATE SHAKE.
AT NO EXTRA COST, THAT GETS YOU A TRIPLE BYPASS AND A PORTABLE DEFIBRILLATOR TO GO.
R. SCHLEMME

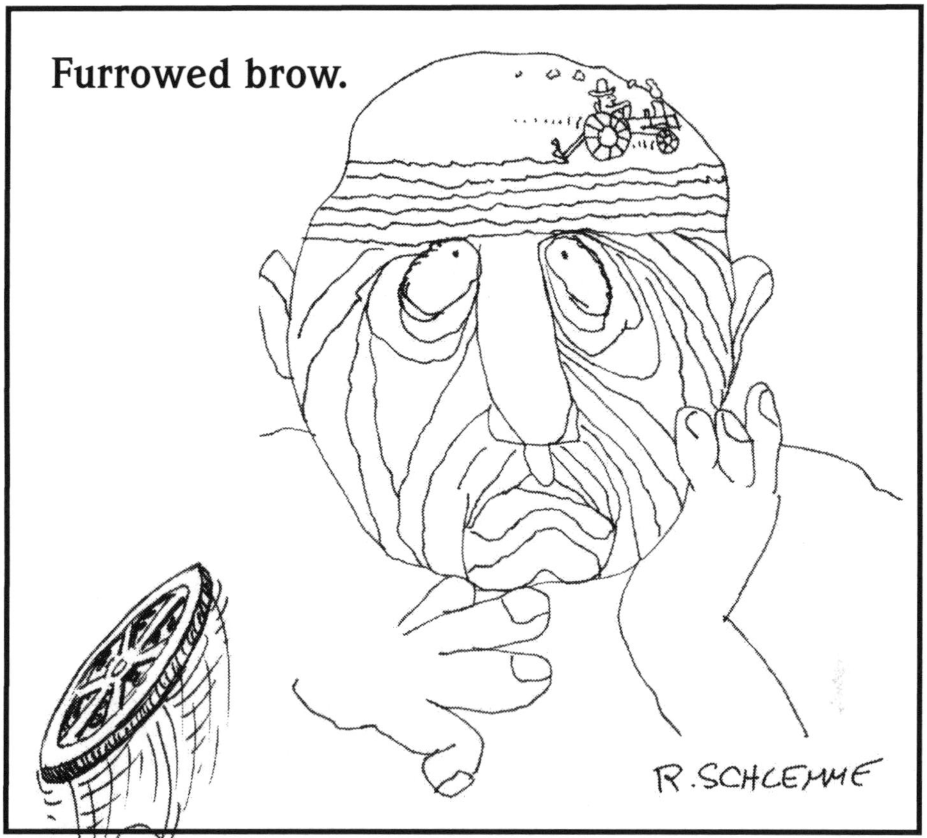
R.SCHLEMME

Furrowed brow.

"Call it!"

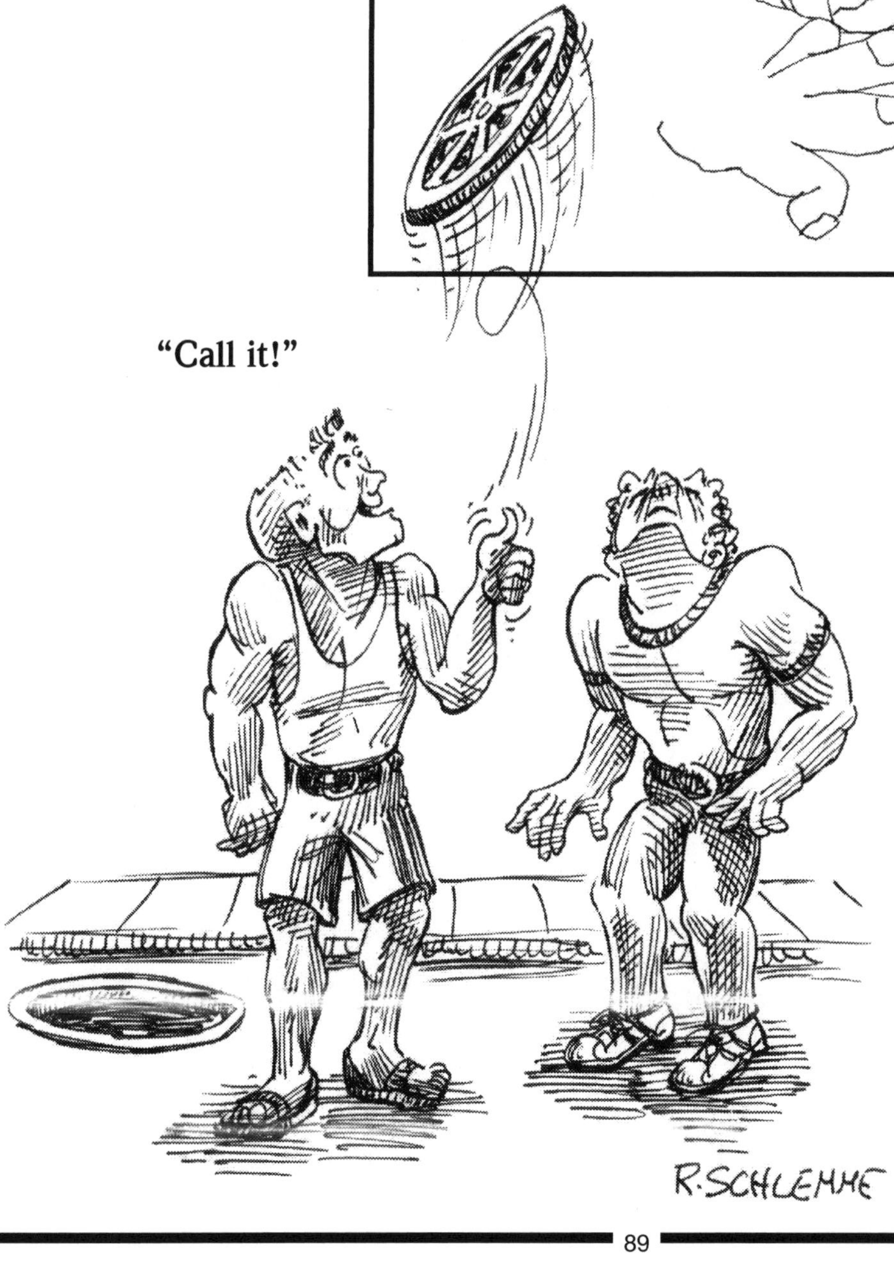
R·SCHLEMME

"Sorry, Mom and Dad...I just feel there's
a greater need for CPAs out there."

"Wake up and come to bed!
It's half past Charlie Rose!"

R. SCHLEMME

"Hey, Merle! That book from
'The Land of Great Concepts' just came.
Now you can be a social philosopher 24/7!"

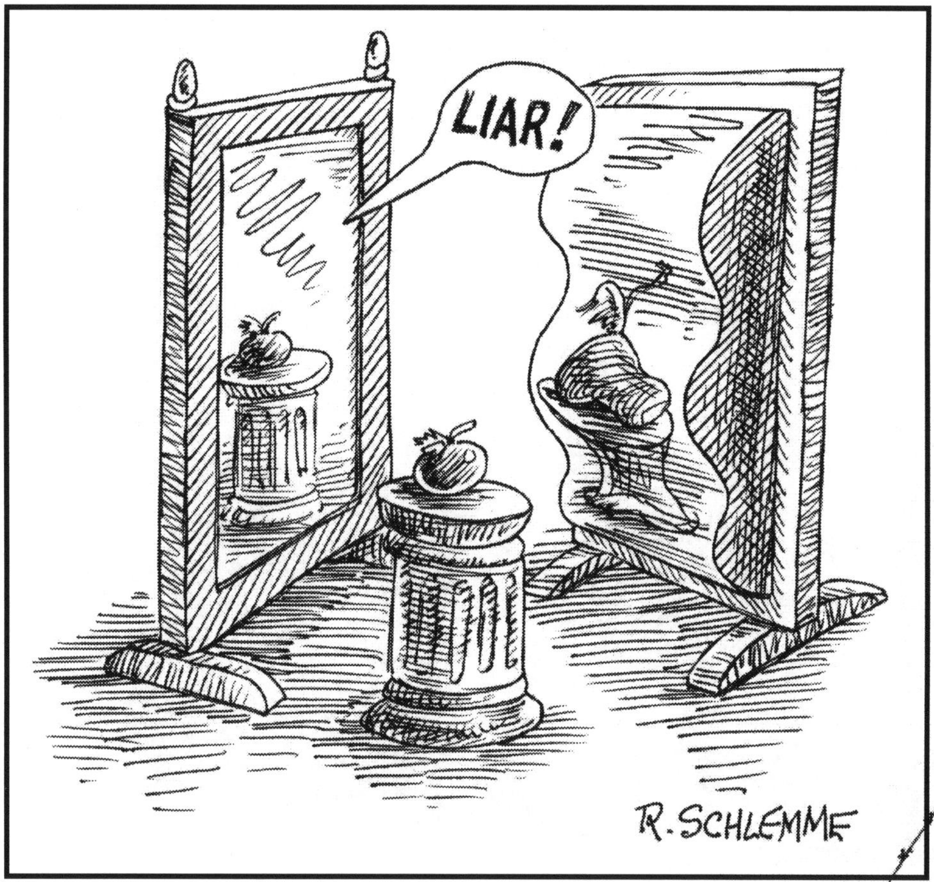
LIAR!
R.SCHLEMME

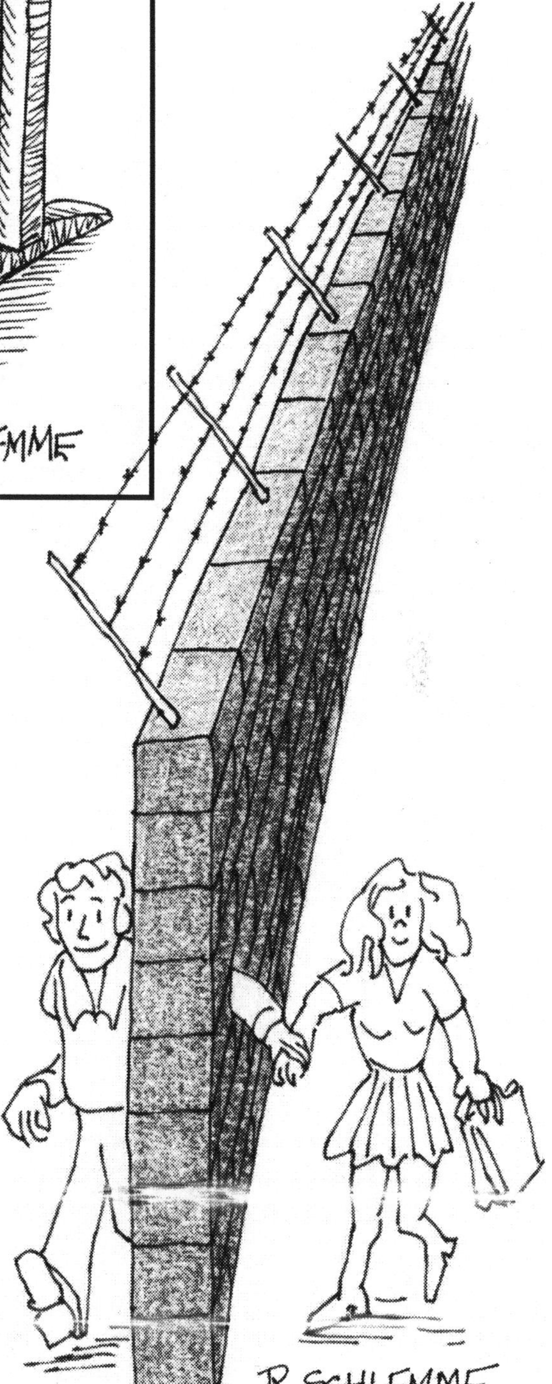
R.SCHLEMME

"Remember my warning, Jim?
All meds carry the risk
of side effects."

R. SCHLEMME

"I really hope our suite's 'awesome view'
is worth a half-hour trek to get there."

"Sorry, we're all out. What's your second choice after *'Nectar of the Gods'*?"

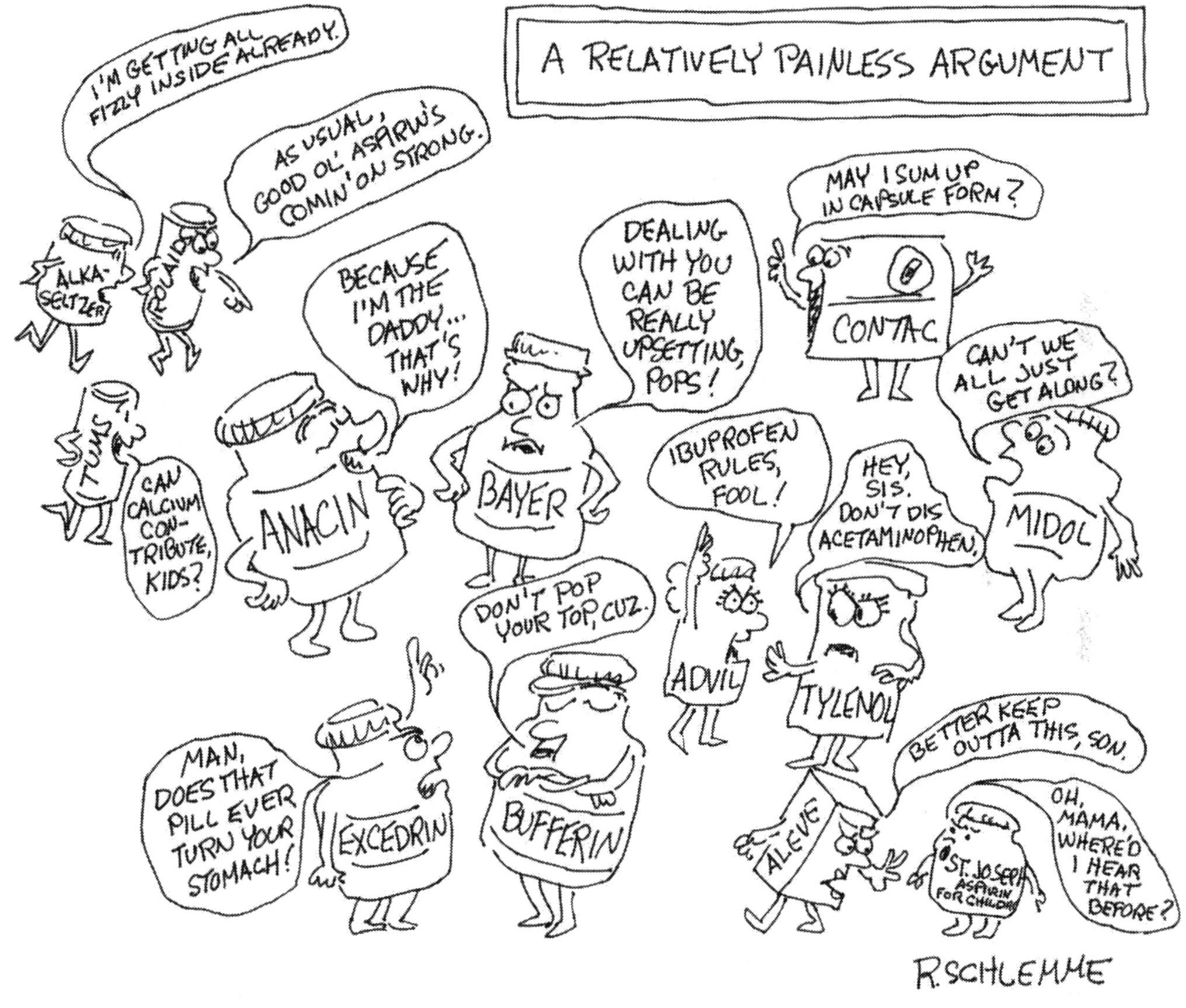
A RELATIVELY PAINLESS ARGUMENT
I'M GETTING ALL FIZZY INSIDE ALREADY.
AS USUAL, GOOD OL' ASPIRIN'S COMIN' ON STRONG.
ALKA-SELTZER
ECOTRIN
MAY I SUM UP IN CAPSULE FORM?
CONTAC
DEALING WITH YOU CAN BE REALLY UPSETTING, POPS!
BECAUSE I'M THE DADDY... THAT'S WHY!
TUMS
CAN CALCIUM CON-TRIBUTE, KIDS?
ANACIN
BAYER
CAN'T WE ALL JUST GET ALONG?
MIDOL
IBUPROFEN RULES, FOOL!
HEY, SIS. DON'T DIS ACETAMINOPHEN.
DON'T POP YOUR TOP, CUZ.
ADVIL
TYLENOL
MAN, DOES THAT PILL EVER TURN YOUR STOMACH!
EXCEDRIN
BUFFERIN
BETTER KEEP OUTTA THIS, SON.
ALEVE
OH, MAMA, WHERE'D I HEAR THAT BEFORE?
ST. JOSEPH ASPIRIN FOR CHILDREN
R. SCHLEMME

"Whatever trifling details future historians
aren't aware of, won't hurt them."

"Get real! Who, in our world,
isn't a horse's ass?"

"Au contraire, mon ami...I happen to feel
this town _is_ big enough for the both of us."

REJECTED NETWORK PILOTS

© R. SCHLEMME

THE ROSE GARDEN

...SO REMEMBER, NOBODY WITH SIX LEGS GETS IN TO SEE THE CHIEF.

PLOT: MID-EAST TERRORISTS CREATE & RELEASE GENETICALLY ALTERED GIANT APHIDS TO THREATEN THE PRESIDENT AND HIS WHITE HOUSE STAFF. WEEKLY CAMEOS BY FADING SHOW BIZ PERSONALITIES AS GUEST EXTERMINATORS.

What's My Twinge?

MY HEAD HURTS! MY FRONT HURTS! MY BACK HURTS! MY TAIL HURTS! MY SOCKS HURT!

PREMISE: FACED BY A VARIETY OF WHINING HYPOCHONDRIACS, OUR PANEL OF PRICEY MEDICAL SPECIALISTS DIAGNOSES AND TREATS THE MYTHICAL AILMENTS USING ONLY THOSE PRESCRIPTION MEDICATIONS TOUTED ON PRIME-TIME COMMERCIALS.

THE WORD WRESTLING FEDERATION SPELL-DOWN

SLAM! S-E-L-M! WRONG! R-A-W-N!

PREMISE: AN EXCITING COMPETITION AMONGST SOME OF THE WORLD'S GREATEST PRO ATHLETES SHOWING THEIR SPECTACULAR KNOWLEDGE AND MASTERY WITH WORDS OF ONE SYLLABLE AND LESS.

THIS OLD SPOUSE

OUT TO LUNCH AND BREAKFAST AND DINNER

PLOT: A WEEKLY MANSION HUNT BY HIS WIFE AND GROWN CHILDREN TO GUESS THE ROOM IN WHICH THEIR FAMILY'S OCTOGENARIAN PATRIARCH CURRENTLY FINDS HIMSELF DISORIENTED.

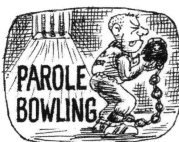

PAROLE BOWLING

PREMISE: INTER-PENITENTIARY TOURNAMENTS IN WHICH WINNING TEAM MEMBERS EARN BONUS POINTS TOWARD REDUCED SENTENCES AND APPEAL HEARINGS. ACCORDING TO PENAL STATISTICS, NOT A SINGLE PAROLEE HAS EVER BEEN KNOWN TO COMMIT A CRIME WHILE BOWLING.

AMERICAN IDLE

I CAN'T ARGUE WITH THAT!

PREMISE: THE DESPERATE POLITICAL SEARCH BY DISGRUNTLED VOTERS FOR A VIABLE 'CANDIDATE OF THEIR DREAMS.' EVERY FOURTH WEEK DEVOTED TO INTERVIEWING EXTRATERRESTRIALS AS 'POSSIBLES.'

THE THIN DEAD LINE

...AND HAVE A NICE DAY.

PLOT: A TENSE DRAMA IN WHICH QUEUED BANK CUSTOMERS, UPON SEEING THE LONE TELLER ON DUTY PITCH FACE DOWN AT HER WINDOW, MUST QUICKLY DECIDE WHETHER SHE HAS DIED SUDDENLY, OR IS TRYING TO SUBTLY ENCOURAGE EVERYONE TO USE THE ATM.

THE ANIMAL WHIRL SURVIVOR GAME

PREMISE: ENDANGERED SPECIES POPPED INTO A MAYTAG AND SUBJECTED TO A 10-MINUTE SPIN/DRY CYCLE. THOSE HARDY ENOUGH TO SURVIVE ARE AWARDED MILLIONS FOR PRECIOUS HABITAT PRESERVATION. THOSE THAT DON'T, GET A FREE TRIP TO ALPO-LAND.

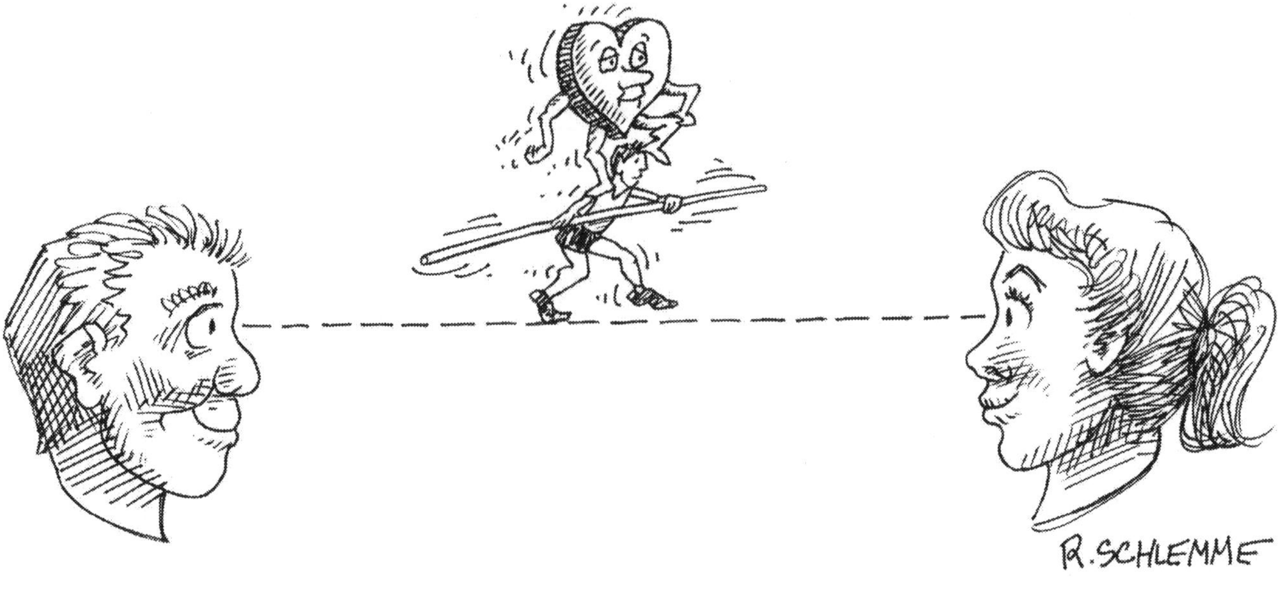
R.SCHLEMME

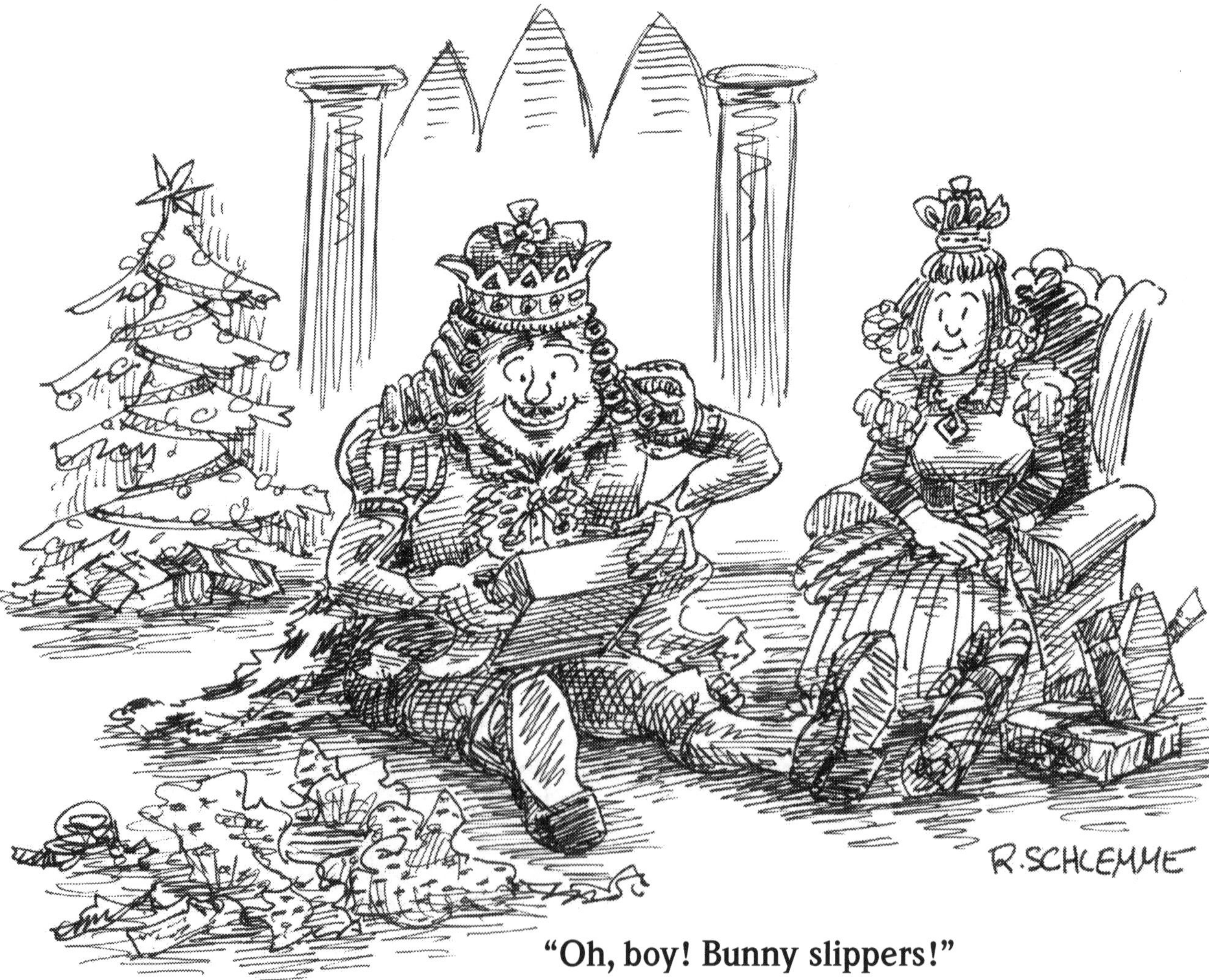
R.SCHLEMME

"Oh, boy! Bunny slippers!"

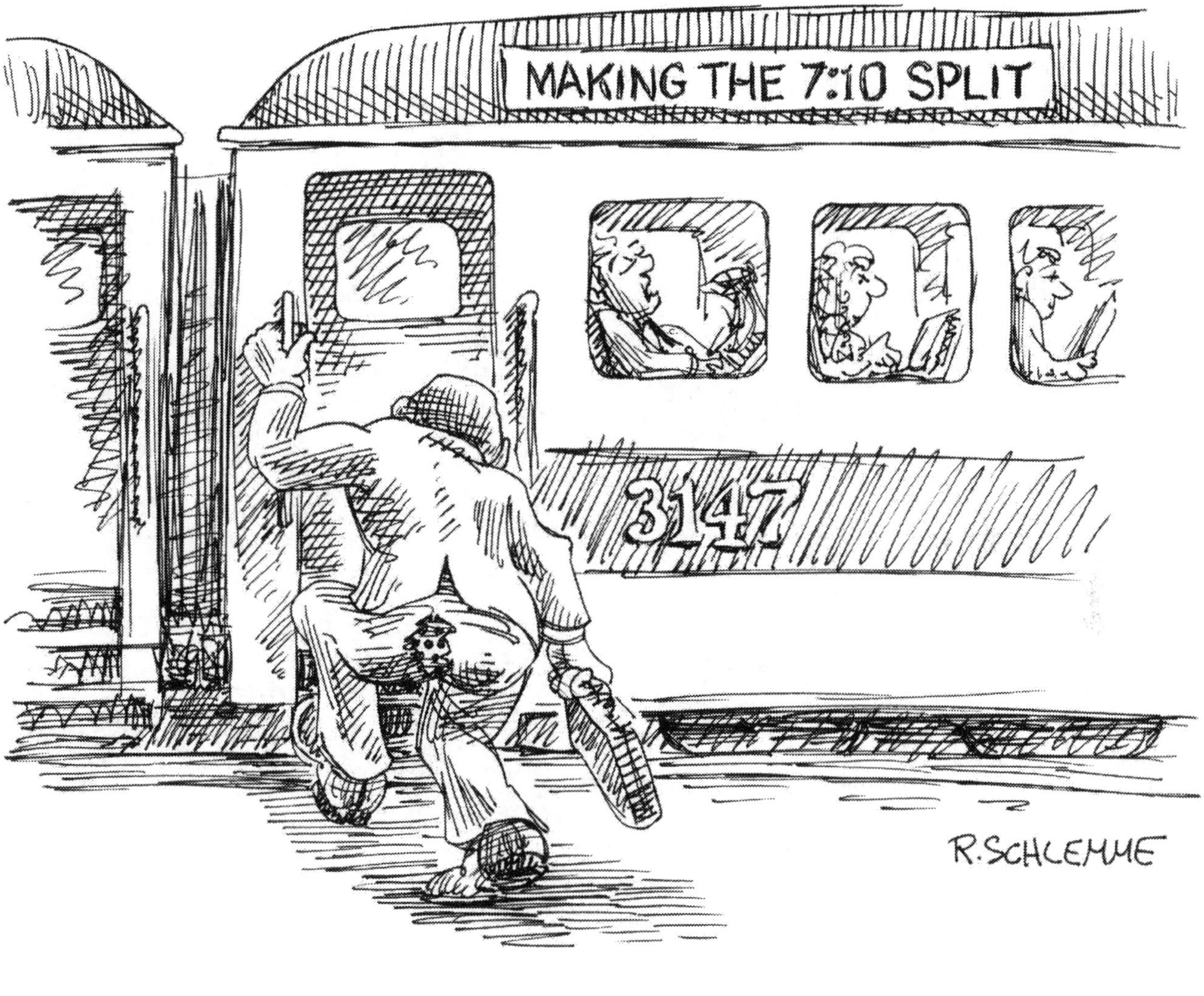
MAKING THE 7:10 SPLIT
3147
R. SCHLEMME

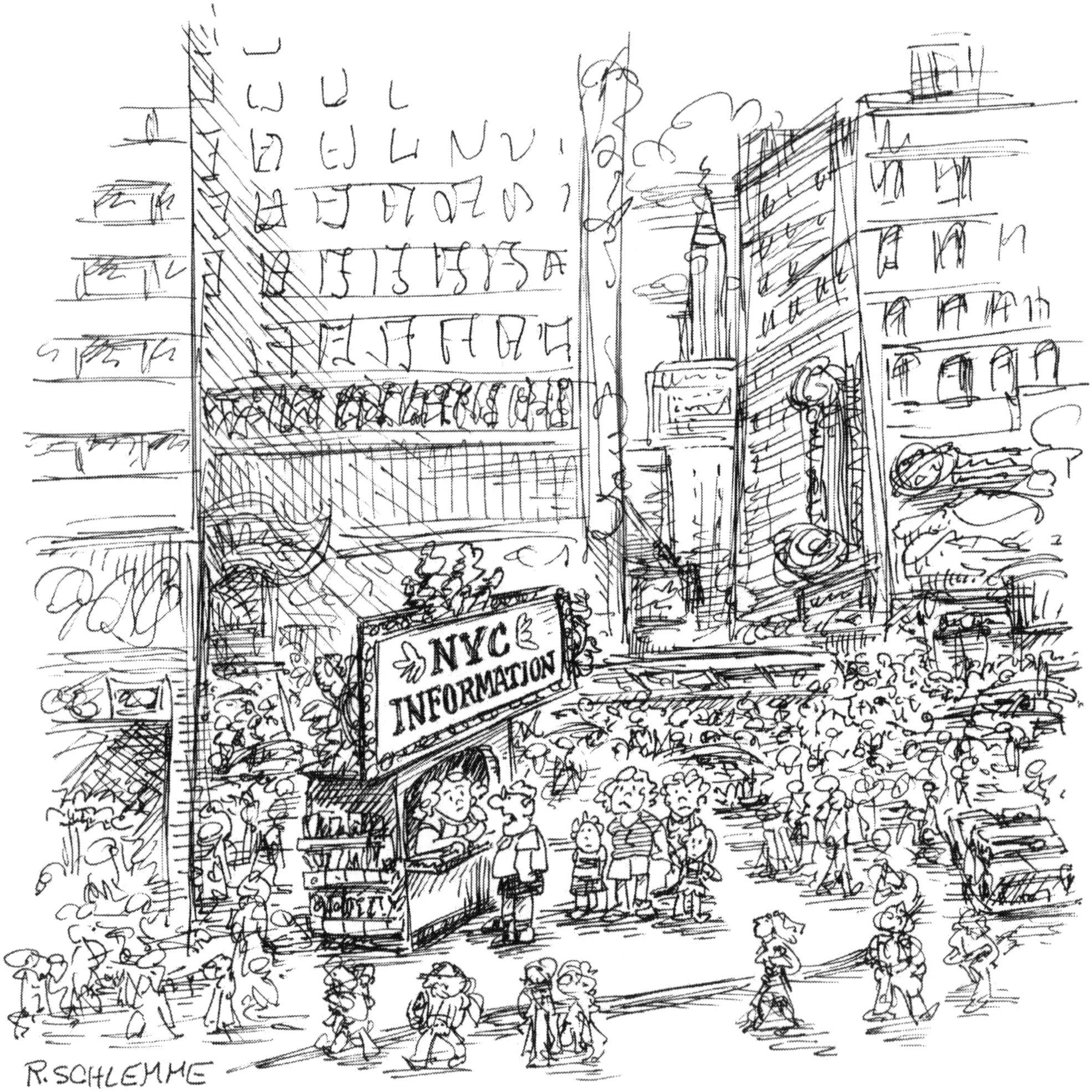
NYC
INFORMATION
R. SCHLEMME

"Where's *'The Quiet Zone'*?"

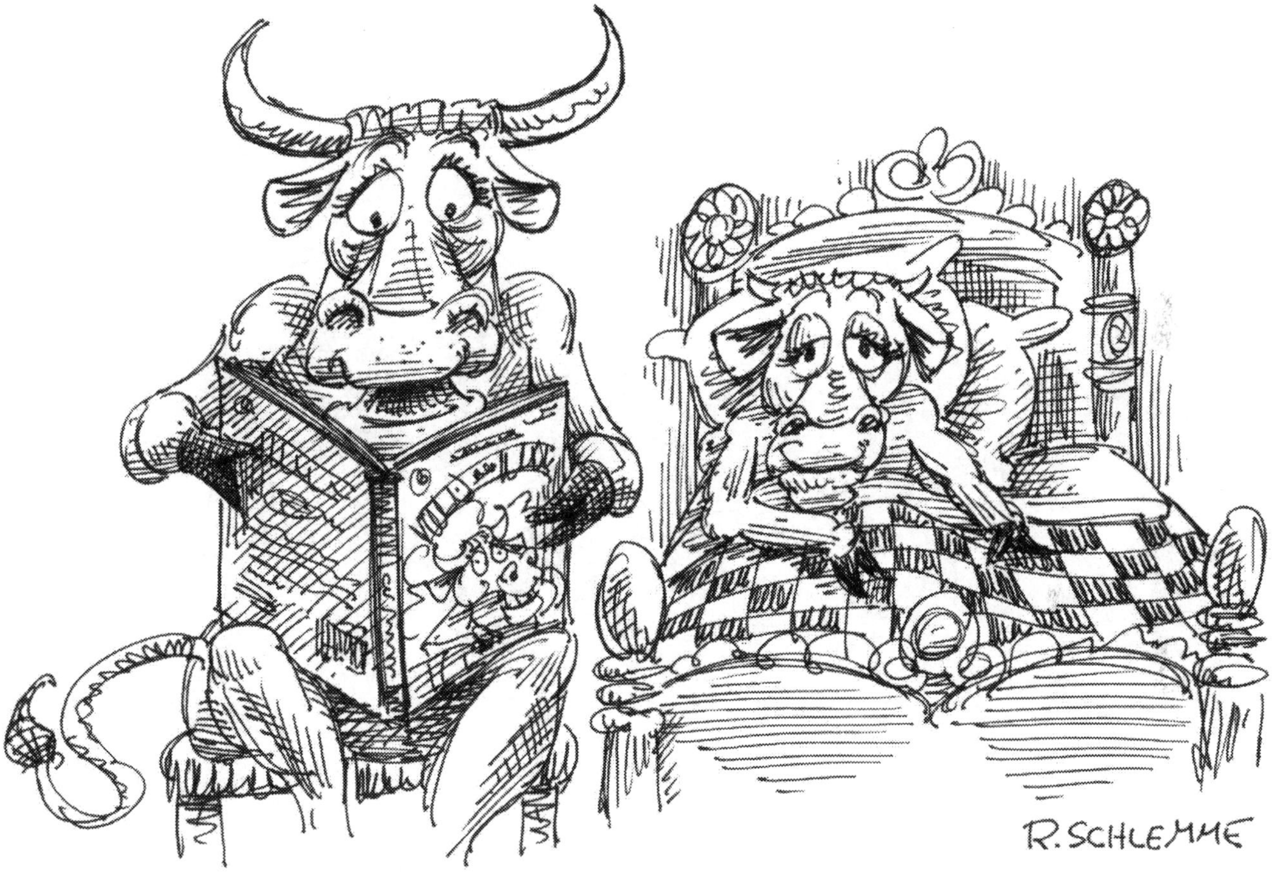
R. SCHLEMME

"Then, after picking up the banderillas, Mighty Toro began to chase Little Matador all around the bullring."

"The Gods reveal you as a great and generous soul
easily able to afford an extra fifty drachmas
for a quality chicken entrails reading."

Deceiving appearances.

R. SCHLEMME

"I smell the insidious handiwork
of an ad agency here!"

"Funny, out there in the wild you never notice how cute these little suckers really are."

"Smooth swing. Nice follow-thru. Total focus.
Ever consider a pro golf career?"

"I'm always amazed by how much
kids can grow in just a few months."

R. SCHLEMME

"Harry, check out our supply of brimstone."

"Got any openings on your
dance card after my BP test, stud?"

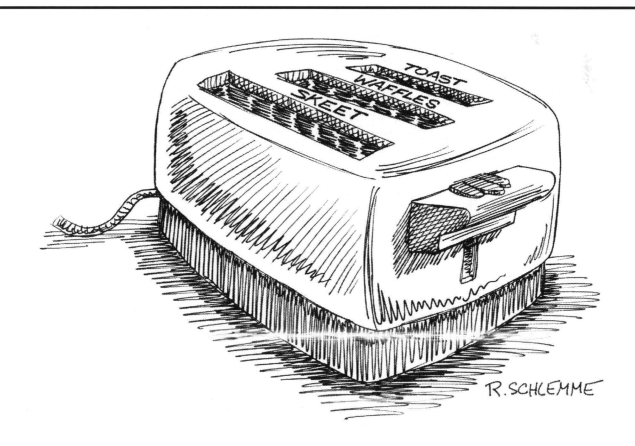

EARLY MAN BOWING DOWN TO A FALSE GOD.

Breakfast with an industrial designer.

"At this late point in my career,
what possible difference could it make?"

The boy who ignored 'hornet' stories.

"Back off! No 'chair repair' wishes!"

"My advice? Keep plugging.
There's no way things liven up until
you connect with some new outlets."

"Damn! Our cover's blown! I forgot
about today being 'Dress-down Friday'."

"Anybody here able to beat
three eights and a pair of derringers?"

"I'm taking the kids out for a little air, hon."

R. SCHLEMME

"The health benefits are great,
but I do it mainly to crack open nuts."

"Let's review. It's 5 points for a 'head hit',
7 for his abs and a big 10 for..."

R. SCHLEMME

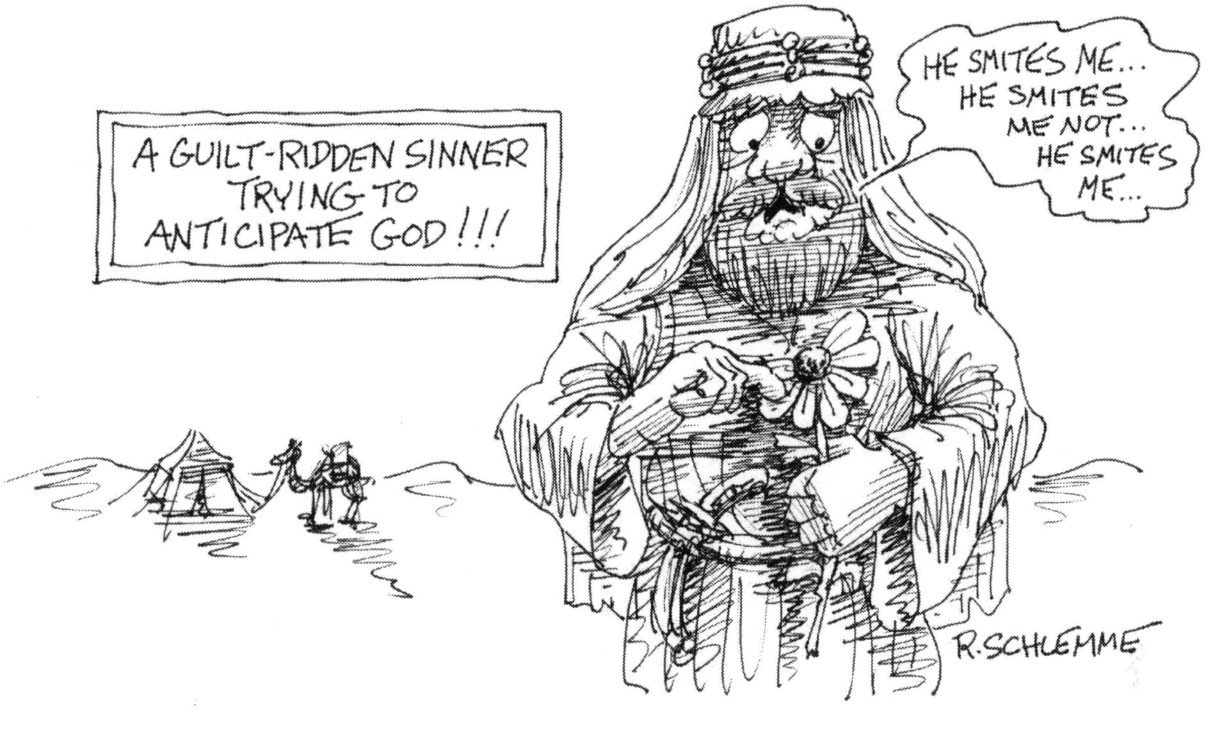
A GUILT-RIDDEN SINNER TRYING TO ANTICIPATE GOD!!!
HE SMITES ME... HE SMITES ME NOT... HE SMITES ME...
R. SCHLEMME

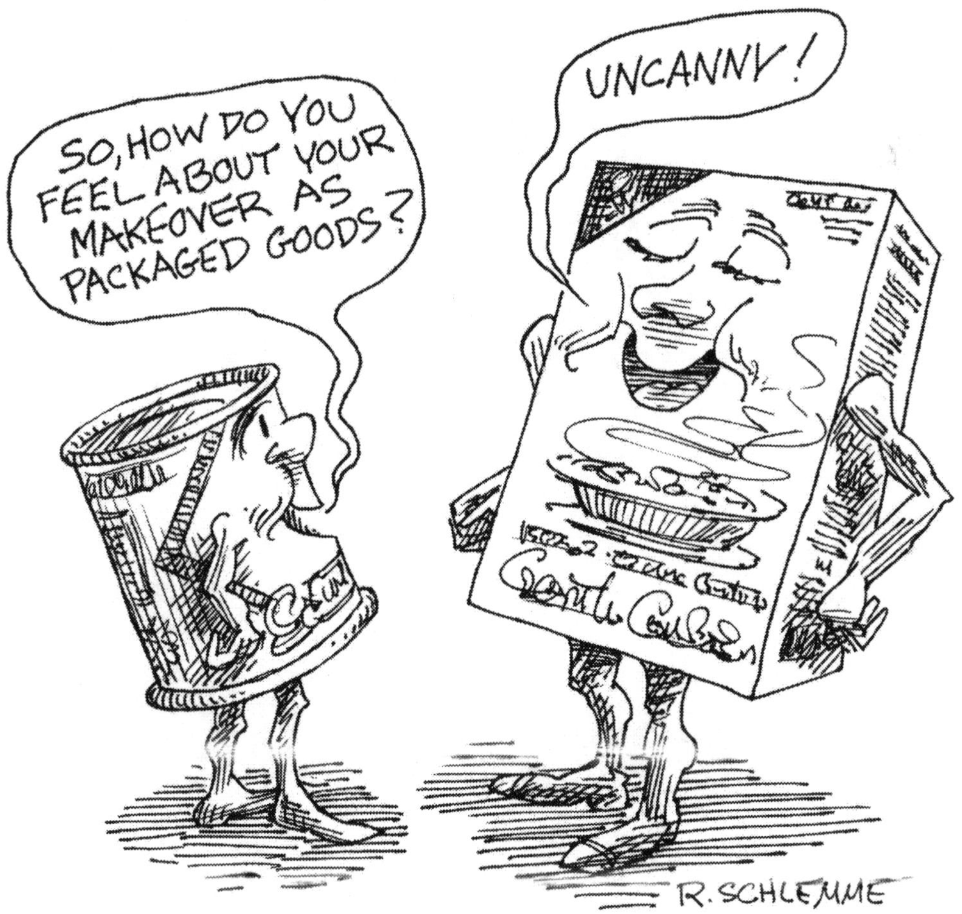
SO, HOW DO YOU FEEL ABOUT YOUR MAKEOVER AS PACKAGED GOODS?
UNCANNY!
R. SCHLEMME

"Yes! Expanded and
improved news coverage!"

"Been grazing over by the power line again, eh?"

"It's OK to take a 'hiccups' break."

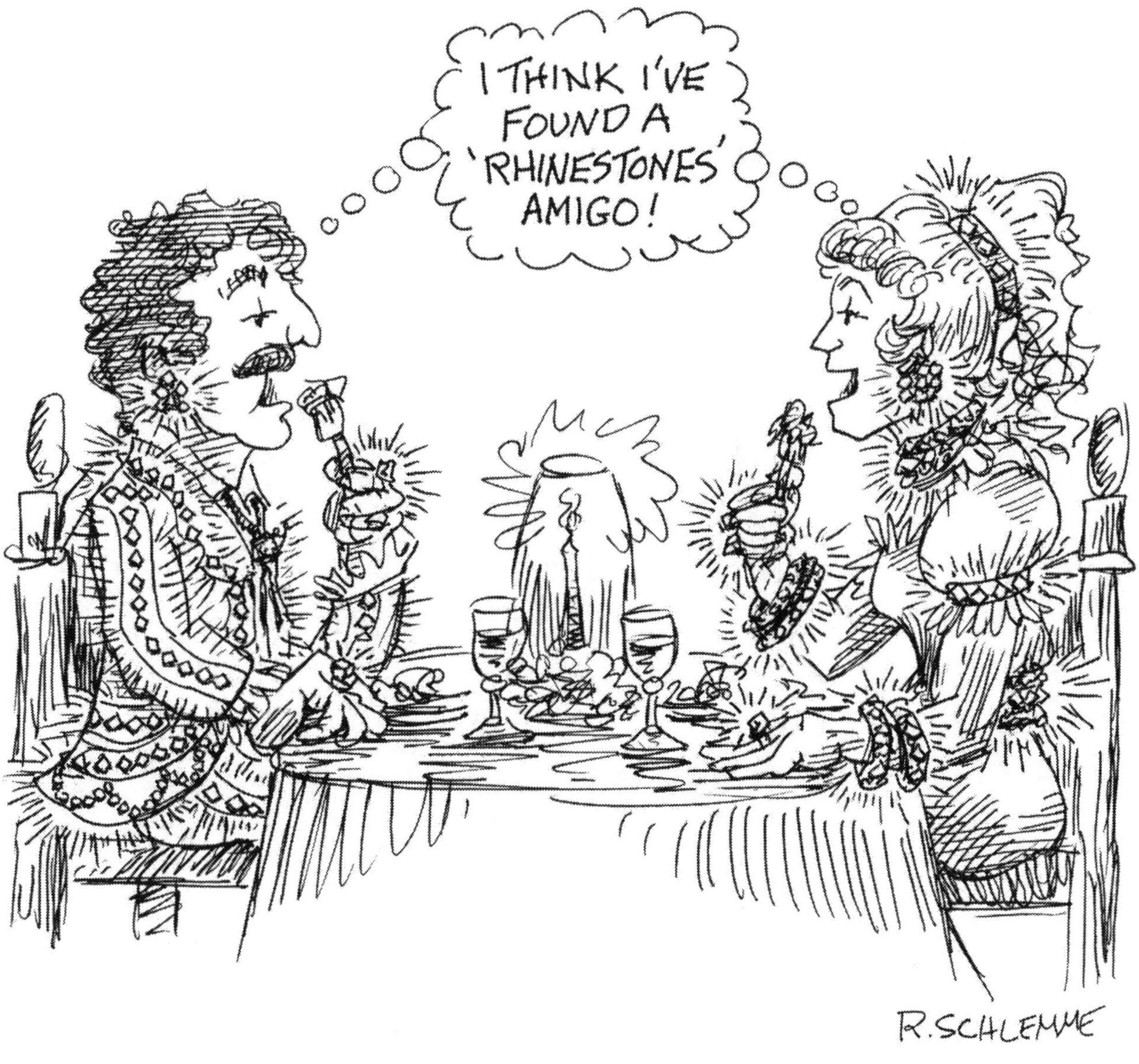
I THINK I'VE FOUND A 'RHINESTONES' AMIGO!
R. SCHLEMME

Union Pacific-1
Trackless prairie protector-0

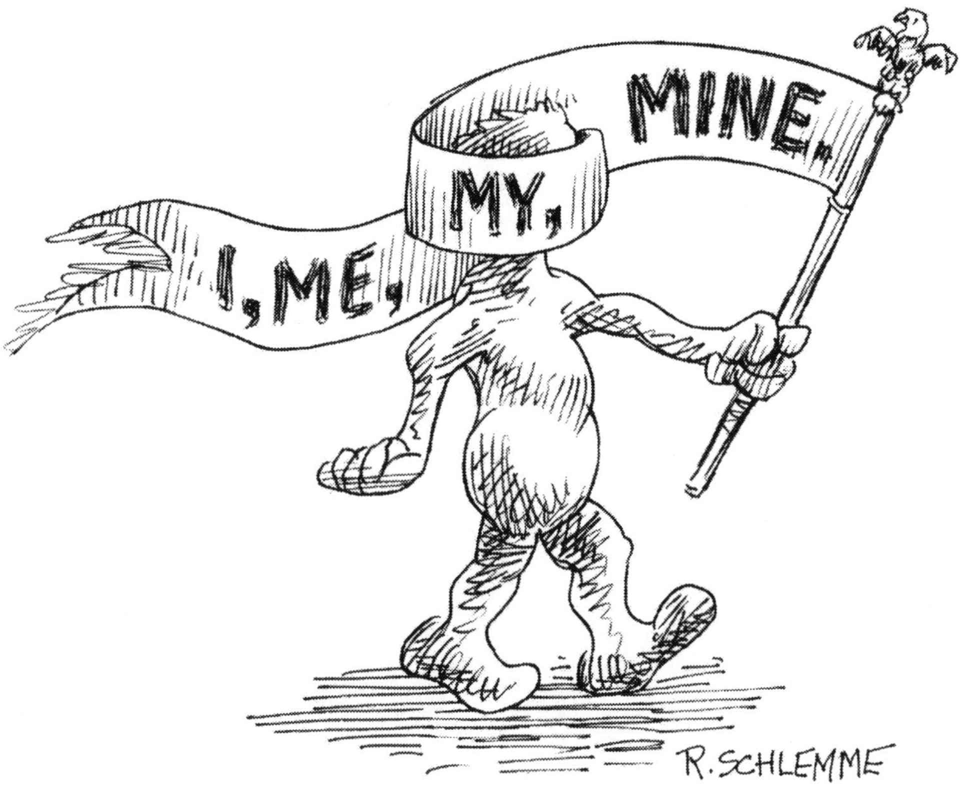
I, ME, MY, MINE.
R.SCHLEMME

So ends the visual hodgepodge of a creative ego!

...or maybe not. Presumably, you've enjoyed Roy Schlemme's oddball humor in *Men's Suits! 25% Off!*, or you wouldn't have gotten this far (unless you're one of those antsy readers who always skips to the last page to see how things turn out). Good news! There are currently six other Schlemme cartoon books, all available through AuthorHouse. For more specific information, check the back cover.